49 - 52 - 53 - 56
58 - 62 68 70
72 - 76 - 77
        idea of "squaring"
79 charter 80
    134

No. 8
Brief Lives
CECIL RHODES

Brief Lives

CECIL RHODES

CECIL RHODES

By
ANDRÉ MAUROIS

Translated from the French
by Rohan Wadham

BRIEF LIVES
COLLINS, ST JAMES'S PLACE
LONDON

PRINTED IN GREAT BRITAIN
COLLINS CLEAR-TYPE PRESS: LONDON AND GLASGOW
1953

CONTENTS

* 1 *

Background to South Africa

THE LIFE of Cecil Rhodes is part of the history of South Africa. It is therefore essential to describe the country before considering the man.

The southern half of the African continent is like a top balancing on a rather blunt point. This huge top consists largely of a rocky plateau of sandstone and granite skirted on the east by a great chain of mountains, the Drakenbergs. Only a narrow strip of land lies between the steep face of the mountains and the Indian Ocean. It takes the full blast of wind and rain from the sea. Farther inland, on the plateau, the climate is dry and healthy, the air invigorating because of the altitude. But along the coastal strip, which drains all the water from the Drakenbergs, the vegetation is almost tropical, the climate oppressive.

The central plateau, with its low rainfall, is a steppe, designed by nature for herds rather than crops. Its scrub is the home of big game, from the

7

antelope to the rhinoceros, the hippopotamus to the lion. Farther west lies a completely rainless area surrounded by mountains—the Kalahari Desert.

In the country as a whole there are few navigable rivers, for the largest are broken by waterfalls and rapids. The coast provides no natural harbours. So it is hard to land on the continent in the first place and still harder to penetrate the interior in the second. It is for these reasons that the colonisation of South Africa was late in starting and slow to develop.

The primitive tribes, who inhabited the country under the rule of their chieftains, were Bushmen, Hottentots, Kaffirs and Bantus. When the first Europeans landed, the Bushmen, who had lived for centuries on the brink of starvation, were still in a Stone Age; the Hottentots, who were stronger and more numerous, knew something of refining metal; while the Bantus, who comprised Basutos, Bechuanas and Zulus, collectively called Kaffirs (The Unfaithful) by the Arabs, were in still larger and more developed groups ruled over by powerful kings.

Until as late as the sixteenth century the black races were left by the Europeans in sole possession of South Africa. In 1486 the famous Portuguese explorer, Diaz, had discovered the Cape; in 1497 Vasco da Gama sailed round it. Diaz had christened it the Cape of Storms, but King John II of Portugal renamed it the Cape of Good Hope. The explorers had noticed Table Mountain, the strange flat-topped mountain which commands the Cape, and Table Cloth, the white cloud which invariably hangs over it. The poet Camoens wrote of this semi-Atlas who seems to stand guard over the edge of the world and, by a strange coincidence when one thinks of subsequent events and the name that was to figure so much in them, compared it to the Colossus of Rhodes. The Portuguese attempted a landing in 1510, were attacked by the Hottentots and turned to a plateau on the east coast which they called Mozambique, as a base and revictualling point.

Towards the end of Queen Elizabeth's reign the English and Dutch began to compete with the Portuguese for the Indian trade.

They had to break their journey, which took six months, at a port of call. The Cape was inviting. The English made an abortive attempt to establish themselves there and fell back on the small island of St. Helena. About the middle of the seventeenth century the Dutch East India Company, learning that some shipwrecked Dutchmen had come to terms with the natives at the Cape, and that the fruit and vegetables, which they would need for revictualling their ships, grew splendidly there, determined to make it the half-way house they sought. In 1652 a Dutch surgeon, Jan van Riebeck, and his companions landed from three small ships. They built a fortress near a swamp full of wallowing hippopotamuses ; the Hottentots sold them cattle and promptly stole them back again; English and French ships threatened them. It was a hard and precarious existence.

For all that the colony flourished. Five hundred French Huguenots joined the original Dutch settlers following the revocation of the Edict of Nantes. Dutch orphan girls came out to look for husbands, and not surprisingly found them. Black slaves were transferred from Mozambique to work in the fields. The climate was excellent and the Boers (the Dutch word for peasants) became moderately prosperous, but their progress was retarded by the severity and greed of the Dutch East India Company and its appointed Governor. A number of Boers tried to escape from his dictatorship by moving northwards, but came up against the natives and had to abandon the attempt.

By the end of the eighteenth century the colony contained about sixteen thousand Europeans, farmers who enjoyed a simple and domestic life, practised an austere fundamentalist creed and resented any interference from the Governor. The more adventurous of them took their cattle over the mountain barrier which encircles the Cape. They found themselves much happier in those great expanses of country, so essential to their cattle, which had always to be on the move in search of fresh grazing.

Then came the wars between England and revolutionary France, and in 1795 Lord Elphinstone took possession of the Cape in the name of the Prince of Orange, who had been chased out of Holland by the French. For strategic reasons England had to prevent French squadrons seizing the Cape. But when the Dutch became Napoleon's allies England herself annexed the territory as a colony. In 1814 she acquired the legal title to the Cape on paying Holland six million pounds, and by 1820 English settlers had begun to arrive.

The first Governor was Lord Charles Somerset. The Boers hated him, partly because he was officious, partly because they, as nomadic shepherds, refused to be governed, but above all because he supported missionaries whose aim was to evangelise, and by degrees emancipate, the natives, whereas the Boer, with his prejudiced outlook on race, held them to be congenitally inferior. The creation of a native police force succeeded in infuriating the colonists, who thought a Kaffir should never so much as touch a white man.

In 1833 the Abolition of Slavery Act reached the Statute Book and in 1834 the Act was applied to South Africa. Such a measure cut straight into the racial pride of the big cattle breeders on the northern frontier. In addition it affected their interests since it deprived them of cheap labour. Thirty-nine thousand slaves were set free and it seemed to the Boers that misery and ruin stared them in the face. Furthermore, they were hurt by the introduction of English instead of Dutch as the official language and at seeing the local magistrates, whom they had been in the habit of electing, replaced by meddlesome officials, who were powerless to protect the frontier against Kaffirs because of the huge distances. In short, these earnest Bible readers, in whom the idea of mass exodus was implanted by Holy Writ, finally resolved to leave the colony and to found an independent state. They were prepared to fight for a corner of the world in which they would be free to enjoy self-rule.

Their exodus came to be known as the Great Trek. The verb " trekken " in their language meant to heave, to harness the oxen or to move on to new pastures. The nomads were subject to " trekzucht," the urge to be on the move which had always stirred the Boer. Before the end of the century some isolated bands had already trekked, but the Great Trek of 1835-1836 stood out through the numbers of its pioneers. Nearly ten thousand set out. It was an extraordinary sight. Whole families travelled in long wagons painted red, green and yellow, and each drawn by fourteen to eighteen oxen.

By slow degrees they crossed the wide plateau, the arid veld. The harnessed oxen and the herds, driven on by horsemen with long whips, had to find their food as they went. Each night the procession was drawn up in a circle, like a barbarian encampment, to ward off the attacks of tribesmen and wild animals. The Boers were superb shots who feared nothing and no one. Taciturn and strict masters of their families, these patriarchs had little use for neighbours. Their migration would have been like the wanderings of the ancient native tribes had it not been that the Bible was their spiritual guide. The children of Israel were once more on the road to exile.

The Great Trek was split into several parts, for, as we have already seen, vast grazing grounds were needed for the herds on this bare plain. Some of the Boers established themselves on the near side of the Orange and Vaal rivers. Among these was a boy of eleven, Paul Kruger, who never forgot the early struggle. Their leaders, Potgieter and Pretorius, had driven before them the native tribe who inhabited the region, the Matabeles. Then, again inspired with " trekzucht," and having to move on, they followed the Matabeles over the Vaal (hence Transvaal) and established themselves in this

hitherto unexplored area. They imagined that here
they would be left in peace by the Cape Government.
Other Boers spread out to the east and, reaching
the top of the Drakenbergs, found the enchanted
plains below them; the warm, fertile and vernal
plains of the narrow strip between the mountains
and the sea. This was the land that Vasco da Gama
had originally called Natal (*terra natalis*) because he
had discovered it on Christmas Day, 1497.

Occupying Natal were a Zulu chieftain and his
tribesmen as well as a certain number of English
colonists under their local governor at Port Natal.
The Zulus, supported by the English, attacked the
Boers, but after heavy losses on both sides the
invaders conquered and set up their first independent
republic, Pietermaritzburg. At first the British
Government showed no concern about these subjects,
who were flouting her authority, but disagreement
arose between the Dutch and the English of Port
Natal. The natives became involved and in 1842
British troops were sent to Port Natal. Shortly
afterwards Natal was declared a British colony by
Sir George Napier, Governor of the Cape.

The Boers were not strong enough to resist, but,
having made the Trek and paid for their liberty in
blood, they were not prepared to owe allegiance to
the Crown again. They made their way back through
the Drakenbergs and attached themselves to the

roving Boers now dispersed over vast areas to the
north of the Orange and Vaal rivers. Here they
noticed that the community was not organised for
administration or defence. The pastoral life, which
puts such distances between one herdsman and
another, is hardly conducive to the creation of
government. For all that two small republics, the
Orange Free State and Transvaal, were founded at
this time. They were reminiscent of the Hebrew
Kingdoms, whose history was conjured up for the
Boers, by their nightly Bible readings. They too had
their Amalekites and their Philistines, represented
by the Kaffirs and Zulus. These natives, half Arab
and half Negro, were warlike but chivalrous.

In 1848 the British intervened, to protect the
native tribes and to secure the frontiers of Cape
Colony. Pretorius put up some resistance, but after
a brief struggle the Orange Free State was annexed.
Once more the trekkers decided to move on and
crossed the Vaal. For a time it looked as if the
Dutch cattle breeders by their hard struggle against
the natives had done no more than pull the chestnuts
out of the fire for the British administrators in the
Cape. But in London a Liberal Cabinet was
opposed to colonial expansion. Parliament deplored
the added expense and responsibility it involved,
which showed no signs of a quick return. The
Governor's action was not supported and two envoys

were sent to treat with the Boers. In 1852 Britain recognised the independence of the Transvaal and in 1854 that of the Orange Free State. The two countries were reconstituted as republics under their Volksraads, parliaments elected by "Burghers," Dutch farmers and traders.

At the same time Cape Colony was endowed with representative political institutions. Since 1827 the colonists had had the right to trial by jury and had clamoured for an elected assembly. Now, in 1854, they were granted a constitution. It was a three-tier system composed of the Governor, his Council, who were nominated by him, and an Assembly elected by landowner suffrage. This Assembly had some powers, in that it voted the budget, but the Governor and his Council were not responsible to it. Many reforms were to be introduced before the Cape became a free country.

Thus, when the young Englishman, whose extraordinary adventures we are about to describe, landed in South Africa in 1870, this great land mass consisted of five states or territories; two Boer republics, the Orange Free State and the Transvaal; two Crown Colonies, Cape Colony and Natal, and vast native territories, Kaffirland and Basutoland, over which England exercised a vague protectorate. Kaffirland had a population of one thousand whites and ninety thousand natives. " The ship was English, the passengers Kaffir, Hottentot and Zulu." In the whole of South Africa there were three million natives and less than four hundred thousand whites. Agriculture and cattle breeding were almost the only sources of wealth. The fearless, wild and warlike tribes were a continual threat.

At this time the Boers lived on farms of about five or six thousand acres, of which not more than fifty would be under cultivation. The farmhouses were large barns with plain earth floors. The farmers were hospitable people, though midnight revels were hardly the rule. Their literature consisted entirely of a Dutch Bible and some books of psalms. When a young man wanted to get married he would mount his horse and set off for a neighbouring farm carrying crystalised plums and a wax candle. The plums were for the girl's mother, the candle for the girl. If she accepted him it was immediately lit, and the mother retired, sticking a large pin through the wick an inch or two below the flame to set a limit upon the young couple's courting. The Boers only drove to the towns, Pretoria and Bloemfontein, to go to church. They were austere and brave, scornful of recent Dutch settlers and hard on their slaves. As to foreigners, they were suspicious of them and tried to avoid them.

In 1867 an extraordinary discovery was made.

At the northernmost point of Cape Colony and the Orange Free State, and near the river Orange, a certain Schalk von Niekerk noticed some children on Jacob's Farm playing with very luminous stones. He asked if he could buy one, and was given one instead. He met a trader, called O'Reilly, and asked him to have the stone examined. O'Reilly promised to, left the stone behind in a hotel, recovered it again and at last gave it to an expert, who recognised it as a large diamond worth at least £500. Two years later a tribal witch-doctor brought von Niekerk his charm. It was a giant diamond which fetched him five hundred sheep, ten oxen, and a horse, and which, when cut, was to become the " Star of South Africa."

London jewellers were at first sceptical. One expert, Mr. Gregory, stated simply, " No sign of diamond-bearing soil in South Africa." To this day a really bad gaffe is known in the Cape as a Gregory. But before long the doubters were forced to recognise the facts. In 1869 beautiful diamonds were found on the river bed of the Vaal, and in 1870 on the land of a farm called Dutoitspan, where searching was far simpler than on the river bed.

Now the ' Rush ' began. The place was hard to reach. It was seven hundred and fifty miles from the Cape and five thousand four hundred feet above sea level. It could be reached from the Cape or from Port Natal. From the Cape it took six days by stage coach across the flat, bare, scrubby veld, dotted with the carcases of oxen on which the vultures preyed. One arrived exhausted, with swollen legs. It was a hideous journey, but there was no shortage of adventurers and they arrived from every corner of the globe. They were amazed by the mirages, which were as common as in the Egyptian desert, by the herds of ostriches and by the Kaffir and Hottentot villages. When they reached diamond fields such as Dutoitspan, where dry digging was begun, Old de Beers, named after the Dutch farmer who had sold the land, or Kimberley, they dreamt of making their fortunes overnight.

In 1870 there were already five thousand prospectors: by 1871 there were thirty-five thousand. This raised serious political problems. To whom did this Eldorado, whose wealth exceeded the legendary mines of Golconda, belong? Originally, it had been occupied by Griquas, a mulatto tribe of Dutch paternity and Hottentot maternity, who were led by a certain Waterboer. Then the Boer farmers of the Orange Free State had taken possession. The resident English official in Bloemfontein had agreed to this, but under conditions which assumed their full importance as soon as diamonds came into the picture. The half-caste Waterboer had got hold of

a wily lawyer and was making himself out to be the owner of all the diamond-bearing fields.

In August 1870 the President of the Orange Free State summoned Waterboer and told him that the Orange Republic was beyond doubt the sole proprietor of the mines. Waterboer put himself under the protection of the British Government, who hastened to grant it to him. The Governor of the Cape warned the prospectors, who were mostly English, to resist the claims of the Boers; dispatched a British official and finally made the seven hundred and fifty mile journey himself. It was worth the trouble, as the whole question had become thoroughly involved. Concessions had been granted by people who were not proprietors; letters had been written by a chieftain who could not read; title deeds had been effected by long possession.

But Sir Henry Barkly, the Governor, had not come all this way to get entangled with legal niceties. He had been enthusiastically received by the proprietors, and when the President of the Orange Free State summoned a " commando " of a thousand men to support his claims by arms the Governor warned him that it would mean war with Great Britain. It was a sufficient warning and shortly afterwards the Colonial Office authorised the Cape Government to undertake the administration of Griqualand. So it was that when the Rhodes brothers, to whom we shall now turn, arrived in Kimberley they found themselves on British territory.

* 2 *

From Hertfordshire to Kimberley

CECIL RHODES, one of the few men to have given his name to a country, was born on 5 July 1853, at Bishop's Stortford in Hertfordshire. Before the Norman Conquest the Manor of Stortford had been sold by Eddeva the Fair, the wife of King Harold, to the Bishop of London. William the Conqueror had confirmed the gift. The grammar school was founded in the reign of Elizabeth. So we can see that Bishop's Stortford was a town hallowed by tradition and that its living, which fell to Cecil's father as vicar of Stortford, was one of some importance.

The Reverend F. W. Rhodes was descended from Cheshire farming stock. As his son was later to put it, " I believe that my ancestor was a keeper of cows." The father was a kind and generous man, but rather eccentric, overbearing and obstinate. It was one of his idiosyncrasies that he made his sermons last exactly ten minutes, not a minute more, not a minute less. He had many children, including seven sons, all of whom he would have liked to see in the Ministry. As it turned out, four of them became officers and three of them colonists. As for Mrs. Rhodes, born Louisa Peacock, she was a well-bred and attractive woman whose sister, Aunt Sophia, became the real confidante of her sons. "My mother," Cecil said later, "got through an amazing amount of work: she must have had the gift of organisation, for she was never flustered and seemed always to have ample time to listen to all our many and, to us, vastly important affairs."

Cecil, the fifth son, attracted little attention as a boy. He was fair, pale and reserved. "A grubby little boy with ruffled hair." He developed early a habit of brooding on the serious things in life. His brothers called him "long-headed Cecil." In a family album he gave his answers, at the age of thirteen, to a questionnaire: "What is your motto?" we read. "To do or to die," is his reply. It reminds one of Victor Hugo, who, at the same age and to a similar question, had answered: "To be Chateaubriand or nothing." But the ambitions of Cecil Rhodes were not literary. He dreamt of power and wealth; his thoughts turned first to the Bar because it was more lucrative than the Church. But his father disliked lawyers and Cecil soon gave up the idea. Another of his answers expressed the opinion that celibacy was preferable to marriage. He stuck all his life to this opinion.

Cecil was not a brilliant scholar, but he had " a love for thoroughness." All his life, he was fond of recounting an incident that happened when he was a boy. He went on a visit to a retired Admiral who was about eighty and found him planting acorns. It struck him that his old friend would never see the trees and, somewhat boldly, he said to the Admiral: " Why are you planting acorns, Sir, when you cannot expect to see them growing into trees? "

" My boy," replied the Admiral, " I have the imagination and I already see them as trees, with people walking under their shade. . . . I have the pleasure of the conception of their glory."

Rhodes always said that the lesson had been of the greatest value to him and taught him to build for a distant future he would never see himself.

The Vicar of Stortford sent one of his sons, Herbert, to Winchester and another, Frank, to Eton. For economic reasons Cecil had to be content with the local grammar school. He was making normal progress there when his parents suddenly became alarmed about his health. He was sixteen when he showed serious signs of being consumptive—a tendency to which the family was prone. It was decided that his schooling should be continued in the country and he was packed off to his aunt.

Sophia Peacock lived in a small country house, where she gave parties for the children of the local gentry. Her nephew found with her the same quiet and dignified atmosphere that he had left at home. While he was with her he learnt to ride and became, what he was ever to remain, a very indifferent horseman. But he also took careful note of the arts of farming and became imbued with the ways of the parson and squire which were then so characteristic of the English countryman. All his life he retained a love for the rôle of gentleman farmer, settled but active, possessing a sense of duty as well as of his own authority and always out to see justice done. At this time it seemed as if he would follow in his father's steps. He wrote to his Aunt Sophia that next to law he thought a clergyman's life the nicest. Fate decided otherwise.

In 1870 he was seventeen and had to think of his future in the light of his health. His eldest brother, Herbert, daring and adventurous, had already been a planter in Natal for a year. It was thought that the journey and the change of climate would do Cecil good. Precious Aunt Sophia lent him £2000, no mean sum with which to furnish a young man, and he embarked. He had few regrets at leaving home; many a younger son was going off to the colonies at that time and, as he said himself at a later date, " Why did I come to Africa? Well, they will tell you that I came on account of my health, or from a love of adventure, and to some extent that may be true, but the real fact is that I could no longer stand the cold mutton." Cold mutton was just a symbol and the young man slightly cynical.

The journey took seventy days, which was quick for the times, and on 1 September 1870 he landed at Durban, on the south side of the bay of Port Natal. The rainy season was just ending; the climate was healthy and the country an enchantment. Twenty-five years earlier the place had been a jungle where elephants roamed in herds. Now a town, laced with flower gardens, was rapidly climbing up the hillsides. Herbert Rhodes had not come to meet his brother off the boat. He was on a prospecting trip. Dr. Sutherland, Surveyor-General of Natal, and his wife, met Cecil on his arrival. One might think it alarming for a mere boy to find himself alone at the end of the earth. But Cecil was perfectly self-possessed; he made some friends, found some books, read a lot, and when at last his brother turned up in December, set off with him for a farm he had bought in the Umkomanzi valley.

Herbert was very different from his young brother, " a tall, lean, hatchet-faced man; a restless being;

a stormy petrel, ever on the wing seeking adventure."

The place was not devoid of beauty, vegetation grew profusely in the valley, but it was hot, damp and uncomfortable. The farm only consisted of two cabins, which were both looked after by a Kaffir servant. The ground had to be cleared with native labour. Herbert wanted to grow cotton, which was said to flourish in this rich, virgin soil, but the first crop failed. It was eaten by caterpillars and insects; monkeys raided the plantation. Cecil brought his method to bear. He spread the cotton shoots farther apart and had the brainwave of planting a patch of maize at intervals of eighty feet to attract the insects and entice them away from the cotton. Thanks to this ingenious device the second crop was a success and the Rhodes brothers even won a prize with it at an agricultural show.

There were a few other English people in the district, including one, Hawkins, who was related to the Provost of Oriel College, Oxford. Hawkins lent Cecil his books. He acquired a liking for Latin and Greek and resolved to complete his education at Oxford as soon as he had made his fortune. He was laying the foundations of this fortune by putting part of the small capital given by Aunt Sophia into a railway that was being built between Durban and the Cape. Meanwhile the farm showed only modest profits and Herbert, who found the life of a cotton-planter irksome, learning that diamonds were still being found at Kimberley, decided to go there. He went by himself, leaving his young brother in charge of the farm. In October 1871 the reports from Herbert encouraged Cecil to join him. But his year on the land had not been wasted. His health had improved; he had learnt to combat natural obstacles—and human ones as well—and how to handle the natives. To have produced an exhibition crop after only one year was a miracle. It had given him a new self-confidence. Later in life, when objections were raised to any plan of his, he used to say, " Ah, yes! They told me I couldn't grow cotton."

At eighteen this young man, setting off in his ox-wagon on several weeks' trek to rejoin his brother in Griqualand, was already something out of the ordinary. A practical dreamer. A " shy and solitary spirit," yet capable of making friends. A reader of Plutarch and Plato, who had made up his mind to be both and at the same time a great man and a rich man, a rare and difficult combination. He had to cross a range of mountains, a vast and scarcely inhabited steppe, and organise provender for himself and his beasts: an astonishing programme for a youth who, two years before, was sitting on a classroom bench at Bishop's Stortford Grammar School.

It was a difficult but enthralling journey and crossing the Drakenbergs was magnificent. As he approached the summit near Mount Basuto the huge plains of the Orange Free State stretched out before him. Passing from the virgin forests and jungles of Natal to the clear, invigorating air of the veld stimulated him. Then came the unbroken plateau covered with prickly pear and bathed in a light as changeable as the seas.

These great areas were sun-baked and uncultivated. Here and there was a Boer farm or a " kopje," a ridge of sandstone supporting a flat-topped hillock. At night a prairie fire would occasionally throw the horizon into sharp relief. In the evening light, Rhodes would try to read Homer and Aristotle.

At the end of a month he reached Bloemfontein, the capital of the Orange Free State. Here at last was a town and a hotel. But he soon took up his monotonous trek again and at last, from the high ground overlooking the camp, he saw a mass of tents spread over the wide plain. It was Dutoitspan. The first fires were being lit; before long the plain was dotted with them and Rhodes dropped in with the diggers returning from work with their tools slung over their shoulders. This was a strange city, with no houses. Solicitors' offices, hotels and shops were all in tents; there were only miners and brokers at dinner passing bundles of diamonds from hand to hand. They talked about an Irishman who had bought a bad " claim " for one pound and, in the first day, had found a diamond worth £3000. The hotels were turning travellers away and many new arrivals were sleeping in the open—in the rain. Flies and fleas crawled everywhere.

The next day Rhodes pushed on to Kimberley and found his brother, who had staked three claims. How this was done needs some explaining. Everyone had a right to prospect. As soon as anyone found some diamonds other prospectors rushed towards the new " placer," followed by bakers, canteen keepers and brokers. The newcomers each selected a plot, thirty-one foot square, which they marked out with posts to establish their claim. In the first place it was their only title of ownership and they had to defend it, if need be by force, as there was nothing to stop an interloper seizing the claim, while the original owner was having his lunch, and maintaining thenceforward that he had laid out the posts himself. It was no easy matter to show proof to the contrary.

But as soon as a real diamond field had been discovered and a reasonably large community established, the prospectors set up a committee to execute justice, to draw up charts and to decide when a claim could be regarded as abandoned. From this point onwards possession was not decided by force. Whoever wanted a claim had now to buy it from the owner for a sum which varied according to the nature of the ground and the results already obtained. If these had been outstanding the claim might fetch four, or even eight, thousand pounds. So that, when the rush had been going on for a year, making one's fortune in the mines had become a hazardous affair. But the Rhodes brothers were not afraid of risks and Cecil did not believe in Chance. He overcame it.

* 3 *

Diamonds

Herbert Rhodes had staked his three claims at Kimberley on a kopje, a small, round hillock, about thirty feet high and two hundred feet across. On this hill alone nearly ten thousand men, black and white, were working on 600 claims. Round the hill sprawled a city of tents. Cecil Rhodes describes the scene to his mother, " Imagine a small round hill at its very highest part only thirty feet above the level of the surrounding country . . . all round is a mass of white tents and then beyond them a flat level country for miles and miles, with here and there a gentle rise. . . . I should like you to have a peep at the kopje from my tent door at the present moment. It is like an immense number of ant heaps covered with black ants as thick as can be, the latter being represented by human beings."

It was hard work. Under the red sand on the surface was the reef of shale, in the middle of which was the yellow diamond-bearing soil, whose colour and consistency Rhodes, in a letter home, compared to Stilton cheese. For every few cart-loads of good soil tons of shale had to be shovelled and carried away. In every claim a strip of ground was left for a path, but as the hillock had become a mass of deep diggings these paths overhung considerable precipices. Occasionally, when a cart went too near the edge, the weight took charge and oxen, or horses, and all went hurtling down to the bottom of the claim on top of the miners. Only the sure-footed mule was really suitable for the work, but they were hard to find. At a later stage, when the paths became useless, the miners set up a cable system with pulleys and buckets to excavate the soil.

At the bottom of the mine the earth was put through a coarse sieve. Occasionally a Kaffir would come on a diamond as he dug with his pick. Then he would take it to his master and get a reward. Up on the surface the earth was first of all beaten with wooden bats to break up the shale, then passed through a fine sieve to remove the dust and finally poured out on to sorting tables round which stood men armed with a kind of rake made of tin, or the remains of an old bucket. They would each draw a lump of earth towards them with their rakes and simultaneously go through it for diamonds.

The sorting was so rapid that a newcomer like Cecil Rhodes could hardly believe that some

C.R.   C

diamonds did not escape notice. But, in fact, the rough diamonds, which did not glitter, were hard to miss. The only danger arose from the negligence of chattering native sorters who threw diamond-bearing earth away under the tables. It had even become a profitable business to buy the rejected earth and sort it again. Children and young Dutch girls earned quite a livelihood at this game, and before long a regular band of " illicit diamond buyers," known as the I.D.B., set about corrupting the natives and caused the miners considerable anxiety.

The reef was unbelievably rich. On average one diamond was found for every fifty buckets of earth. The two brothers saw rough diamonds of every conceivable shape and colour changing hands; white, yellow and blue, some of them perfectly clear and others with black streaks. At Kimberley diamonds were the most ordinary things in the world. It was not unusual to find small, one carat, diamonds which had fallen off the carts, in the roadway. They were to be found in the sand on the top of the ground, where the tents were pitched, and in the gizzards of hens, who liked pecking at these stones. Even cooks were getting rich. Not everyone was making his fortune, but, in spite of disappointments, everyone lived in hope and dug feverishly. " Some day," Rhodes wrote, " I expect to see the kopje one big basin where once there was a large hill." (His prophecy came true, and the kopje on which the Rhodes brothers worked became a huge hollow lined with cable railways.)

The remarkable thing was that Rhodes had adapted himself to the life of a diamond digger as easily as he had to that of a cotton planter the year before. And it was a peculiar and hard life at that. Vegetables were sold by auction at Kimberley and fetched almost the same price as diamonds. Meat was provided by shooting and rearing animals, but the scarcity of vegetables and the unhealthiness of the water, which was sold by the pail, so heated the blood that the slightest scratch would go septic.

Thunderstorms were accompanied by torrential rain and the air would be so charged with electricity that circles of light appeared round the cartwheels, and the hyena skins which were used as blankets emitted sparks. Now and again a red dust storm blew up and the grit cut into the miners' faces.

The men were no less disquieting than the conditions. The vicar's son, brought up in the virtuous English provinces, was living at Kimberley among a heterogeneous and dangerous mob. The rush had attracted sharks of every description—American and Austrian diggers, German traders, keepers of gambling dens, prostitutes, pickpockets. As for the labour it consisted largely of the lazy, mulish and

unruly Kaffirs. They worked as little as possible
and stole as much as they could for the benefit of
the I.D.B. Their great ambition was to acquire a
discarded old gun for a pound or so. Then, with
an ox's horn as a powder-flask, they thought themselves invincible and went round firing into the air
with their eyes tight shut. When a bucket, or even
the smallest pebble, fell on their heads at the bottom
of the mine they invariably feigned death. But Cecil
had already met with them in Natal and, in spite
of his youth, knew very well how to command their
respect and obedience.

In fact it was he, and not his elder brother, who
directed the excavation. When Herbert decided to
return to Natal, to have a look at the farm which
he had still not sold, Cecil carried on alone without
the slightest qualm. His bearing was quite remarkable and it was impossible to resist his authority. He
spoke little and always had a far-away look of deep
concentration, but nothing that went on around
him escaped his notice. When he was pondering
something he displayed a mannerism which stayed
with him for life; it was to rub the little finger of
his right hand, which was anchylosed and doubled
over, up and down his chest. He dressed with complete indifference and when he rode, with that
deplorable seat and his trousers rolled up to his
knees, his friends described him as " Jack ashore."

A letter to his mother shows how quickly he learnt that strange business of diamond digging, sorting and selling. He was already making large sums. " I found a 17 5/8 carat on Saturday; it was very slightly off and I hope to get £100 for it. Does it not seem an absurd price? Yesterday, I found a three and a half perfect stone, but glassy, which I sold for £30. . . . I find, on an average, thirty carats a week. . . . Diamonds have only to continue a fair price and I think Herbert's fortune is made." Cecil was beginning to buy claims for himself. " I average about £100 per week." At eighteen and a half, he had claims valued at £5000 to look after.

Through inclination he had few friends, for he kept apart from the other miners as a whole. The few men to whom he did attach himself were educated Englishmen: Rudd, of Harrow and Trinity, Cambridge, and Merriman, the most erudite and gifted conversationalist in the whole of South Africa. Merriman and he would go off together for long rides over the veld, discussing the future of the mines, the Governor of South Africa or the classics to the beat of their ponies' hooves. Merriman, whose father was a dean of the Church noted for his caustic wit, had also been known to show a sharp tongue. But to this " pleasant young fellow Rhodes " he was friendliness itself. He guessed that the boy was a superman. For that matter all the leading men in the country were taking a lively interest in this young man who read so much, who studied the classics on this lunatic fringe.

For all that even those who liked him most found him odd. Norman Garstin, one of his friends, writes: "As I search my memory for the Rhodes of the early seventies, I seem to see a young man frequently sunk in deep thoughts, his hands buried in his trouser pockets, his legs crossed and twisted together, quite oblivious of the talk around him. . . . He was a compound of moody silence and impulsive action. He was hot and even violent at times, but in working towards his aims he laid his plans with care and circumspection. He was fond of putting the case against himself, and this habit of seeing the other side probably helped him much in his career."

He only abandoned his almost perpetual gravity to perpetrate enormous practical jokes; as when he rang the church bell in the middle of the night and all the miners rushed panic-stricken from their tents. He sometimes went dancing and then danced with all the plainest girls, for, as he said, he was only doing it for exercise. Even as a young man in England he had shown no interest in women. In this human jungle his character was becoming even tougher. Sentimentality did not pay at Kimberley.

He ended his normally short, letters home, ' Yrs.
C.R."—already an imperial signature. He was
becoming avid for wealth and with the money
earned from diamonds, he bought land relentlessly,
so as to let it again immediately to farmers, who
were attracted by the big custom promised by
the camps.

Such important business transactions were carried
out by a lad who was not yet nineteen. When his
brother Frank, a little later, joined Cecil, he was
amazed at what he heard of him. Everybody
eulogised his precocity. " Nobody believes I am
older than Cecil. . . . Mr. Merriman praises Cecil
up to the skies. He says he is such an excellent
man of business. . . . He says most young fellows,
when they get up there and do well, get so very
bumptious, but that Cecil was just the contrary.
Cecil seems to have done wonderfully well as
regards the diamonds. . . . I have not repeated half
the nice things he said about Cecil."

The intensity of the work soon wore him out and
in 1872 he fell seriously ill. Perhaps it was a first
heart attack. He set off with Herbert, while Frank
looked after the claim, on a several months' trek
into the little-known country to the north of the
Orange and Vaal rivers. They crossed Bechuanaland travelling along Missionaries Road, and went
as far as Mafeking, Pretoria and Middleburg.

Herbert interviewed the new gold ' placers ' and they returned to Kimberley by the Transvaal, still travelling by ox-wagon. Through the long day's trekking across the veld, or else in the evenings round the camp fires, Cecil meditated silently on schemes greater than diamond digging. What a country it was that he had just crossed! All the wealth of the Arabian Nights was there; diamonds and gold, the fantastic fruitfulness of Natal and the vast grazing grounds of the Transvaal, with all in all a healthy climate and one designed for white people. Now he was in love with South Africa; he foresaw a gigantic future for her, and a great life's plan was working itself out in him. " For four months I walked between earth and sky, and when I looked down, I said this earth should be English, and when I looked up I said the English should rule this earth."

To hand over the governing of the world to men of British descent . . . that was quite a project for a young invalid. And yet he was already thinking that he might one day become the instrument of Providence for its achievement. And by what means would he build this world? By money. Young Rhodes, dazzled by his rapidly made fortune, slightly perverted by the cynical talk of the ad-venturers at Kimberley, believed that money was all-powerful. He wanted money—a great deal of it

—not for what it would buy, but for the power it conferred.

At the age of nineteen, partly through luck, but largely through hard work and intelligence, though he had not yet amassed a great fortune, he had acquired his complete independence. Yet he did not think that an idea could be translated into fact by wealth alone. Prestige was important too. He was conscious of the power he had gained from his adventure but also of the coarse and abrupt manners, that had necessarily been imposed on him by the surroundings at Kimberley. He realised that he must return home to learn some polish and tact from the old country and to receive at the university the heritage of generations. All in all he had made a good start. He had a goal before his eyes; now he had only to make himself a fitting instrument for the realisation of his dream.

* 4 *

Scholar and Speculator

IN 1873 Herbert Rhodes sold his claims and set out northwards. Cecil was never to see him again. It is known that Herbert played some part in developing the goldfields of the Transvaal, and even became a member of the Volksraad, its parliament. The story goes that he trafficked in contraband munitions between the coast of Portuguese East Africa and a rebellious native chieftain and earned himself a term in prison at Lourenço Marques. In any case it was some time later that he moved on to Nyasaland, where, in 1879, he was burnt to death in his kraal. An explorer, Frederick Selous, broke the news to Cecil. He was broken-hearted and took great pains to erect a fitting memorial.

But this is running ahead, for it was in 1873 that Rhodes returned to England with his brother Frank, who had decided to go into the army. Before leaving South Africa, he entered into partnership with his friend C. O. Rudd and began to buy up claims in Old de Beers, which he described as " a nice little mine." Before leaving, he made some very wise investments in diamonds, claims and land. He certainly also had some capital left to invest in England, for, very soon after his arrival there, he bought at Hampstead a property worth £6,200 and offered Rudd to go halves with him, as this would be " a nest egg," safer than diamond securities. Rudd refused and Cecil sold with a profit of £800. He was not very good at losing money.

For the next five years Rhodes was to move between Oxford and South Africa. He had realised his ambition of matriculating to the University. He had chosen Oriel, Sir Walter Raleigh's old college, about which his friend Rudd had told him so much. He never had rooms there. He was only taking a pass degree as an undergraduate with no special subject. He left the college £100,000 in his will.

He led a secluded life at Oxford. He attended few lectures but read voraciously. The two greatest influences upon him were Gibbon, whose *Decline and Fall* persuaded him that the mantle of the Roman Empire, her responsibilities and privileges, had fallen upon England, and Ruskin's lectures: Ruskin who would say to his pupils, " All that I ask of you is to have a fixed purpose of some kind for your country and yourselves. . . . Will you,

youths of England, make your country again a royal
throne of kings, a sceptred isle, for all the world a
source of light, a centre of peace. . . . This is what
England must do or perish; she must found colonies
as far and as fast as she is able . . . seizing every
piece of fruitful waste ground she can set foot on,
and there teaching her colonists that their chief
virtue is to be fidelity to their country." This was
exactly what Rhodes was aiming at and the master's
rounded phrases were the embodiment of the young
pioneer's dreams on the lonely veld.

Naturally, the returned adventurer, whose experi-
ences were so varied, had little in common with his
fellow undergraduates. " The change from Kimberley was at first rather odd," he says of his
translation from the law of the jungle to the most
civilised city in the world. Older, and far more
mature than the others, he astonished them by his
revelations and shocked them by his cynicism. His
contempt for the conventional and his sartorial
carelessness were held against him. When his tutor
criticised his methods and reproved him for " cutting
tutorials," he simply countered, " Now, Mr. Butler,
you let me alone and I'll pull through somehow."
At the dinner following his initiation as a Freemason
he caused an unprecedented stir by divulging the
secrets of the society. His fellows did not take to
him. They found him too much engrossed with his

own thoughts. As a conversationalist he was inclined to pick on any problem which specially interested him, in an almost childish way, and then to invite everyone else's opinion on it for his own benefit, without opening his mouth again. That was always to be his way. He never bothered to entertain; his object was to prise knowledge out of people, not to amuse them. Although his manner was quite different in Oxford from what it was among his business friends in London, he never, in either place, revealed more of himself than would suit his immediate company. This enabled him to attach himself to people of totally different backgrounds.

His first stay in Oxford was a short one. He caught a chill rowing on the Isis, and his lung trouble flared up again. Years later he happened to see the diagnosis that an eminent doctor had made—" Less than six months." Fortunately, even the eminent fall into error! All the same, before the end of the year, he had to return to Africa, where, as usual, treks and long rides soon put him right.

While he took good care of his health he did not neglect his interests. The diamond mines were going through a bad patch. The rich yellow soil was running out; the shale reef was crumbling; water seeped into the mine; the roadways were turning to mud and it was becoming increasingly difficult to get earth out of the claims. Under the layer of yellow soil lay a blue one, which was said to be barren of diamonds. Many smallholders were selling out.

Cecil Rhodes trusted the intuition that told him that there were as many diamonds in the blue soil as in the yellow. Rudd and he bought for all they were worth. Rhodes realised that the small diamond digger was being overburdened by his expenses, and that the way to reduce these was to amalgamate the claims and eventually to control the diamond market so as to keep up the price. His first move towards his final objective of uniting the mines was to get himself under contract to pump water out of the combined workings. It seemed to be a foolhardy undertaking. Not only had he to persuade all the stakeholders to employ his services, but he had also to procure equipment whose sole owner was unwilling to sell. But Rhodes's tenacity was such that he always succeeded in persuading people to do the very opposite of what they intended. At last he secured the equipment, but at such a price that he could no longer pay for its removal. However, in spite of the uncertainty of the times, a Boer undertook to transport it and accept a cheque in payment. Rhodes never forgot his trust in him. From it sprang his high regard for the Boer character.

The pumping plant he had bought was worn out and broke down. He learnt that a far-away farmer had received a new pump from England. He started at once, with six mules and a cart, intending to buy the plant and bring it back with him. But the farmer refused to sell. Why should he? He had bought the pump because he needed it.

" Yes," said Rhodes, " but I'll give you a handsome profit and you can buy a new one."

" That may be," the farmer said, " but I am not going to sell."

" I will come back," said Rhodes.

He came back, day after day, " squared " the farmer's wife, became a friend of the house and was so insistent that in the end the farmer, tired of discussion, gave way. Rhodes rushed back to Kimberley and was able to fulfil his firm's engagements. It was a triumph of tenacity.

It was at this time, 1874-1876, that a man crossed his path who was attempting to amalgamate the claims at Kimberley, just as Rhodes was doing at Old de Beers. This was Barnett Isaacs, known as Barney Barnato, the son of a Jewish tobacconist in Whitechapel and the grandson of a rabbi. He had come out to South Africa in 1873 to join his brother Harry. They were also a remarkable pair, who passionately loved the theatre and whose spare time was devoted to amateur productions of Shakespeare. Barney's original capital had been exactly sixty boxes of cigars. But cigars fetched a good price in

Kimberley and before long he had left his tobacco stall, bought a horse and cart and become a " kopje-walloper." This meant going round the sorting tables and buying rough diamonds.

The story grew up that Barney's first lessons in the business, of which he knew nothing at the outset, were learnt from the horse, which he had bought from another " kopje-walloper " who had pulled out. The horse used to stop of his own accord at the points where his previous owner had traded. That, at any rate, was the legend at Kimberley. At all events, Barnato made enough money in thirty months to buy a number of claims. But the rivalry between the two men had hardly begun when Rhodes went back to Oxford for the second time.

He seemed now completely cured and for two years, between 1876 and 1878, returned to his spasmodic studies—an undergraduate more different from the general run than ever. On his table would lie those classics which always accompanied him; Aristotle and Marcus Aurelius, their margins covered with notes. Also, grammars and dictionaries and next to them works on pumping and transport and letters to Rudd urging him to " accumulate the ready " for the struggle with Barnato. He was convinced that in a crisis power would be with whoever could lay his hand on cash and buy.

At Oxford he would take examinations and, in the

same week, go up to London and discuss the eventual amalgamation of de Beers and Kimberley with diamond merchants and financiers. When he was in South Africa in 1879 he took part in a punitive expedition against a tribe and amazed his companions by spending the journey deep in a Divinity crammer. He equally astonished his Oxford friends by suddenly pulling a handful of diamonds from his pocket. It was his way of urging them to adopt an active life like his. " Shouldn't do that," he said to a friend who had expressed his desire to become a writer, " It's not a man's work—mere loafing. Every man should have active work in his life."

Some of his friends deplored the double life he led and would have preferred him to stand aloof from the business world. But that would have been out of character. Let us remember he wanted money, not for what it would buy, for his tastes were simple, but for the power it bestows upon a man of political ambition. This did not at all diminish his respect and affection for everything that Oxford stands for. " The Oxford system, in its most finished form," he said, "looks very impractical, yet wherever you turn your eyes, except in Science, an Oxford man is at the top of the tree."

All his life, in fact, he surrounded himself with Oxford men. There was an occasion, years later, when somebody expressed his astonishment at seeing a whole day's finding of diamonds entrusted by him to a single man who carried them off to a lonely hut for weighing and sorting. " Oh! that's all right. He's an Oxford man and an English gentleman." When he was searching for the greatest service he could render to the youth of the Empire he could see none greater than to enable them to go to Oxford. In 1878, he left the university so that he could return to handling his affairs in Africa. But he went back to Oxford several times and ended by taking his B.A. in 1881; although by that time he was a minister in the Cape Government.

It is worth considering him as he leaves for Africa again at the age of twenty-five. Tall and strongly built, he has left his delicate childhood behind. His fair curly hair now verges on the red, his face is rubicund. His mouth suggests energy and decision, but not infrequently scorn and irritation as well. He walks with small quick steps, his toes so much turned inwards that at any moment he might walk on tip-toe. Because he dislikes his own profile he only allows himself to be photographed full-face, and he is careful to keep his hands in his pockets to hide his maimed little finger. For this man, who in many ways is great, suffers from vanity. It is his Achilles' Heel. He is prone, too, to surprising bouts of nerves that make the sight of a boy clipping hedges in his garden suddenly unbearable.

He is not interested in the trappings of wealth. He never wears jewellery and, like a king, often carries no money on him. More than once on a station platform his friends had to club together to buy him his ticket. He needed a lot of food but was not exacting about its quality. He kept himself going on " Biltong," dried meat, but the boats that plied ceaselessly between London and the Cape had to carry a cow and some hens to supply him with fresh milk and eggs.

Doubts have been cast upon his physical courage, his enemies contending that on the veld he always chose to sleep in the middle place in the tent. All the same, as his life shows, he was not afraid of taking risks. None could doubt his moral courage, and he had an inborn power of command. The moment he was struck by an idea he would examine it from every angle and sum up the difficulties so swiftly that the specialists were astonished. His head was full of the details of all his projects and he delighted in cross-questioning his secretaries without warning, insisting that they should give him exact figures. As soon as he had grasped the implications of a decision, he acted without hesitation. He always saw things on a grand scale and, as early as 1877, drew up his first will on a scrap of paper out on the veld. In it he left his fortune to a Trust

" for the extension of British Rule throughout the world."

On religious questions the vicar's son had his doubts. He had read Darwin and believed in the evolution of living things. But that was far from the solution of the problem. The question was " Had God ordained evolution? " Rhodes thought there was an even chance that He had, and that this was sufficient reason for belief in Him, relying, as it did, upon the faith of the individual for the realisation of the Divine Will. And what was God's will? Why, that the English people should fulfill their divine mission of ruling the world to the exclusion of war and for the greater happiness of mankind.

In business, Rhodes believed first and foremost in personal relations—for he knew his own charm and his powers of persuasion. The clue to this persuasiveness was first of all that he used simple arguments, carefully devised for the person he was dealing with, and secondly that his tenacity bordered on the aggressive. He admired the importunate widow in the Scriptures who went from one of her husband's brothers to another, and then through all his cousins, and did not give in until she had moved one of them to pity and marry her.

He was not entirely cynical. He may well have believed that there is one yoke for the lion and another for the lamb, and he was positive that

" every man has his price." He retained an exaggerated idea of the power of money: " Can't you square him? " he would ask brightly. But more than most men he valued the few disinterested friends he had. To them he showed unstinting personal devotion. That was Rhodes in 1878, a compound of prophetic vision, practical experience and ancient learning. It is no ordinary combination and one can justly say of him that " he taught the world a new chapter of the romance of wealth."

* 5 *

"I Want to See All This Red"

ON HIS return to Kimberley Rhodes surrounded himself with reliable friends. Although there was no sentimentality in his make-up he could recognise fineness of character and his closest friends were not men of wealth. They were his secretary and right-hand man, Neville Pickering, for whom he had a great affection; a young Jew, Alfred Beit, the son of a Hamburg merchant whom he later made his partner and who stuck with him through thick and thin with exemplary fidelity, and a young doctor, Jameson, a brilliant live wire who had come to Africa on account of a weak chest. From being his doctor he became his friend, for Rhodes was at once struck by Jameson's valiant nature though well aware of his lack of judgment. These, and a few others, known as the twelve Apostles, had their meals with Rhodes in his " mess," and in spite of his youth looked to him as " The Chief " and shared his faith.

One day at Kimberley, standing before a map on

which Cape Colony, Natal, and the other British possessions were painted red, Rhodes placed his hand over the vast area between the Orange river and the great lakes of Central Africa and said, " I want to see all that red, this is my dream." The difficulty was not simply to paint the map red, but to endow the inhabitants of the continents, as Ruskin had ordained, with Imperial hearts.

Meanwhile South Africa was in fact far more Dutch than British. Out of 320,000 whites there were no more than 100,000 of them English. Ever since Cape Colony had enjoyed parliamentary institutions, the Cape Boers had accepted the *status quo*. As they were the majority they had a feeling of power. Those in the Orange Free State, who were being governed by a wise and moderate President, Brandt, were quite prepared to federate. The Boers of the Transvaal remained hostile. Their President, Kruger, an honest man and a patriot, but an aggressive, astute and distrustful old fox, had not forgotten the Great Trek of his childhood, the flight for liberty.

Kruger was not an educated man, yet he was a strong man, ready to fight for the freedom of his people. He did not want civilisation nor wealth for his Boers, but liberty and the fear of God. " Fearless, ruthlessly virtuous. . . . A man who struck when he was angry but who, with a hunter's wisdom and ·a farmer's patience, was able to wait, certain of divine protection."

The British Colonial Secretary, Lord Carnarvon, who had achieved the federation of Canada, would have liked to apply the same treatment to South Africa. But he ran into obstacles so many and so insuperable that public opinion soon sickened of his long term policy for federation. A stalemate in the Zulu war, the refusal of the Boers to accept the annexation of the Transvaal, Dutch opposition in the Cape Parliament and finally the defeat of British troops at Majuba Hill in 1881, all these were deplorable and Mr. Gladstone, who had replaced Disraeli as Prime Minister, was not the man to persevere in such a struggle. He capitulated and the Transvaal recovered her independence. Kruger was already dreaming of an Africa for the Afrikaners, and in his dreams he in turn was painting the map in their national colours.

Rhodes adopted a sensible attitude to the conflict. Above all he wanted to see South Africa united. "Localism is the curse of South Africa," he used to say. He hoped that Union would be achieved under British patronage, but he had no wish for government from London. Basically it was the idea of a self-governing dominion that appealed to him. He wanted to direct the South African races into working together for the greater good of the Mother

Country; but on a footing of equality. " The Dutch
are the coming race in South Africa and they must
have their share in running the country," he said.
As a candidate for the Cape Parliament he could
have stood for Kimberley, where the English miners
would have elected him triumphantly. But he chose
instead to stand for Barkly West, where there was a
Boer majority, and get himself elected by the
Afrikaner peasants. He was to retain the seat for
the rest of his life—and to order his political life
with as much care as his business. As soon as he
entered politics he bought a large enough share in
a Cape newspaper, the *Argus*, to ensure that his
speeches would always receive the right amount of
publicity.

He delivered his maiden speech in the Cape
Parliament on 19 April 1881, six months before
he got his B.A. at Oxford. Methodical as always,
he took every possible care. Armed with notes, he
spent several hours meditating before delivering the
speech. In an assembly which was making every
effort to imitate the House of Commons, from its
lofty standards of debate and even its Latin tags
to its black frock-coats and silk hats, Rhodes
caused a stir by his deliberate untidiness—" I can
legislate in Oxford tweeds "—and by the striking
violence of his proposals.

He was not an orator in the strict sense of the

word: no measured sentences, neither exordium nor peroration, but little nervous gestures and a halting delivery. But also a conversational tone and a direct approach which went to the heart of the matter and carried conviction. " He took his audience into his confidence," and the mixture of familiarity and authority was very effective. /He offered the Dutch, as he did the English, an ideal which he thought perfectly realisable: a South African federation, self-governing but within the Empire, and, by degrees, extension of the Empire by annexation of native territories. |

His maiden speech had been delivered on the occasion of a native revolt in Basutoland, by the very natives who provided the labour for the Kimberley mines, and his impartiality inspired so much confidence that he was immediately elected to the Commission of Inquiry. He therefore set off at once for Basutoland and there met General Gordon, already famous for his exploits in China and the Sudan, from whom the Cape Government had invited an opinion on the military question.

The conversations between these two outstandingly original men were lively and interminable. When Gordon described how, having subdued the revolt of the Tai-Pings, the Chinese Government had offered him a whole roomful of gold, he added:

" And naturally I refused."

" And you were wrong," said Rhodes, " for it is
no use having ideas without the money for putting
them into practice."

Gordon, who was not easily taken aback, was
stunned:

" I never met a man so strong for his own
opinions; you think your views are always right
and everyone else's wrong."

" I have studied my subject from all sides," said
Rhodes.

" But not from mine," retorted Gordon.

Yet, when Rhodes advised him to negotiate with
the Basutos and not to treat them as their absolute
master, Gordon took good heed of the advice. The
two men were never to see each other again. When
he heard of Gordon's heroic death at Khartoum
two years later, Rhodes said: " I'm sorry I was not
with him." And later he said to MacDonald: " I
liked Gordon. He was cranky in many ways . . .
but he was a *doer*, a man who would move mountains
and gain the objective he had set himself."

It was not long before Basutoland was annexed
by the Cape. This, Rhodes's first political experi-
ment, had been a success. But a matter of far greater
concern was on his mind—the fate of Bechuanaland.
This territory was situated between the Transvaal
on the east and Damaraland and Namaqualand on
the west. It consisted in large part of the Kalahari

desert, but also contained a fertile strip along the Transvaal frontier which provided the only gateway to the north. Through it passed the great commercial road known as Missionaries Road or English Road, the route taken by Livingstone and Gordon. At Kimberley Rhodes had been at the starting point of this route; he had noticed the coming and going of the missionaries and traders, he had driven along it on his trek with Herbert and knew its importance. " I look upon this Bechuanaland territory as the Suez Canal of the trade of the country, as the key to its road to the interior."

From time to time the Boers had made raids on the territory—and had even established two small republics there, Stellaland and Goschen. This worried Rhodes. He considered that at all costs the gateway to the north should be kept open, for the benefit of the Cape and not of London, whose ill-informed policy he dreaded. It was on this occasion that he launched a famous attack on " the Imperial factor." " We must not have the Imperial factor in Bechuanaland. . . . I have ever held one view, the government of South Africa by the people of South Africa, with the Imperial flag for defence." The future was to justify his ideas, but for the time being Rhodes was regarded as a separationist by the Colonial Office.

The Eastern frontier of the Transvaal had been

laid down by agreement, but Boer commandos were
for ever violating it, and every time it happened
Kruger maintained that these were private ex-
peditions over which he had no control. Rhodes
was sent to Bechuanaland and, anxious as always
to find a compromise, tried to negotiate with Kruger.
It was the first meeting between two great men who
were to be at loggerheads for the rest of their lives.
The older man, who was called " Oom Paul " (Uncle
Paul) with respectful familiarity by the farmers, was
as tenacious as the younger. His obstinacy was
celebrated, as was his courage. A story was told
that once when he was hunting big game he cut
his thumb, and then saw the wound was going
gangrenous. He promptly took a knife and cut it
off. He had killed lions in his time and had outrun
the fastest Kaffir runners. Like all his race he loved
to be on trek, to feel wide and free expanses before
him, and it hurt him to see the vice of red on the
map, so dear to Rhodes, tightening round him.

When the two giants met for the first time, in
January 1885, Kruger was about sixty, Rhodes just
over thirty. Both were stubborn. Rhodes was
determined to establish a British federation in South
Africa; the stiff-backed old President was no less
resolved to keep his country free of any foreign
interference and " his people untouched by any

change in the plan of life which they had brought into the country fifty years before."

Rhodes recognised grandeur in a man and admired the originality and cunning of the old fox; he tried to win his confidence, but Kruger had smelt an enemy. " I have not had much schooling," he said, " but I have learnt one thing, to distinguish friend from foe." When Rhodes, having failed in his negotiations, was leaving with some bitterness, Kruger exclaimed, " The race horse is swifter than the ox, but the ox can draw the greater loads. We shall see." He did not have to wait long to see British troops on his frontier. The commandos, over whom he claimed to have no control, were at once withdrawn. Bechuanaland became a British protectorate up to the 22nd parallel. Britain had won, but not, as Rhodes would have wished, by persuasion. For some time he felt a disgust for politics and occupied himself temporarily with his personal affairs only.

* 6 *

Amalgamation

RHODES HAD long known that there was gold in the Transvaal. He had seen deposits of it there with his brother Herbert, but at that time he was fully occupied with diamonds. It was not until 1885, with the discovery of the Rand south of Pretoria, that his attention was really caught. This " Witwater Rand," the White Water Range, was a small line of hills, two days' journey from the River Vaal, on whose slopes extremely rich deposits were found.

Before the year was out Rhodes had sent one of his colleagues to make a reconnaissance. The gold was embedded in a layer of cement. Round nuggets of ore nestled in it but the difficulty of separating the one from the other made exploitation problematical. The great Barnato had been put off by first reports. He refused to have anything to do with it. Rhodes bought the most promising plots and, before exploitation was made infinitely easier by the discovery of how to treat ore with cyanide, and before the discovery of layers of coal near the Rand, he set up Goldfields of South Africa Ltd. in 1887 with his friends Beit, Porgès and Robinson. Although this was an immense undertaking gold was always to remain speculative in Rhodes's estimation. Diamonds were to him a better security. First love always leaves its mark.

A town had grown up near the Rand to shelter the miners—Johannesburg. At first it was no more than a camp, a mass of wretched corrugated-iron huts. But it was not long before a city of stone rose up among the artificial hills, the slag heaps left by the crushers. Its white, yellow and black population was as mixed as it could be, but the English, whether from home, Australia or the Cape, predominated. Other well-represented nationalities were Americans, Germans and Russian Jews. The Boers watched this invasion of "Uitlanders" (foreigners) anxiously. They feared annexation more and more. The English newspapers spoke of it openly and criticised Mr. Gladstone for ever having relinquished the Transvaal to the Boers. At local dinners heated arguments always arose as to whether the first toast should be the Queen or the President.

For his part Kruger was being dangerously intransigent. An ultra-puritan, who only drank coffee and milk, he had brought his rustic habits to the Presidency.

The " Uitlanders," drinkers of whisky, an ungodly crowd, disgusted him. Kruger once addressed a meeting in Johannesburg: " People of the Lord, you old people of the country, you foreigners, you newcomers, yea, even you thieves and murderers . . ."

An unbending man, a xenophobe rather than a nationalist, he detested foreigners, feared being swamped by them, and did not want to grant them any rights at all. Although there were four times as many English as Boers in Johannesburg he would allow them no part either in the state government or even in the town's administration. While to his friends, who were Dutch or German industrialists, he granted monopolies which enabled them to entice labour away from the English mines.

Rhodes went to see him twice to explain the miners' grievances. But Kruger merely grumbled, " Though a man has a million pounds he cannot alter the law." The President considered that the foreigners, far from complaining, should be grateful to the Burghers for having wrested the mines from the natives. Rhodes defended the rights of the English. The conflict of two such wills held all the seeds of catastrophe.

Simultaneously with his struggle with Kruger, Rhodes was still fighting a battle of diamonds with

Barnato. He had Alfred Beit as an ally and associate. When he had wanted to amalgamate all the claims of Old de Beers Rhodes had gone straight to Beit, who owned a large number of them.

" What is your game? " he asked.

" I am going to control the whole diamond output before I am much older," said Beit.

" That's funny," said Rhodes, " I have made up my mind to do the same. We had better join hands."

Rhodes achieved the De Beers amalgamation in 1887 and at once raised the profit margin by cutting down production costs and suppressing theft. The I.D.B. had got to a point where they were buying seven hundred and twenty-five thousand pounds worth of stolen diamonds a year from the native workers. By putting his workers in camps, sealed off from the I.D.B. and the outside world, Rhodes had saved De Beers this annual sum and the company prospered. His own earnings from it were about £50,000 a year at this time.

At Kimberley Barnato had adopted the same policy of amalgamation. He was the richest of them all, displayed a genius for speculation, was backed by a financial house in the city and owed his personal success largely to a lively wit. But he was in a more vulnerable position than Rhodes, for there was a French company which had a considerable interest in Kimberley and in which Rhodes managed to acquire an interest, thus planting a foot in the enemy camp. Besides, Rhodes knew more about mining, whereas it bored Barnato to read about it. " It saves time to hire people to read for you," he used to say. Barnato was thought of as daring, and even reckless, but in fact Rhodes was far more so, and where his big plans for the future were at stake he was entirely ruthless. He was an enemy to be dreaded. He never forgot, he never forgave, and he never gave in.

For his battle with Barnato he had the backing of Lord Rothschild in London. This enabled him to buy up Kimberley shares. But his buying, which raised the share price, coincided with a falling market in diamonds. Tempted by the profit, Barnato's shareholders started to sell out. In 1888 Barnato saw that he was beaten and gave in without rancour. The De Beers group (Rhodes and Beit) had complete control of Kimberley and so the whole production of South Africa was put under the aegis of a new company, the De Beers Consolidated Mines Ltd, a corporation formed with a capital of only £100,000, all the shares, except twenty-five, being held by four men: Rhodes, Barnato, Beit and Stow (one of the Rhodes's early partners). They were life governors and had the power " to issue further shares to be exchanged

for those of old De Beers and Kimberley Central."
In its charter was a clause authorising the company
to take any political action it might think necessary.
Rhodes the business man was cutting out a path
for Rhodes the Empire builder.

The contract was signed after a whole night's
discussion in Jameson's bungalow, with Rhodes and
Beit on one side, Barnato and his nephew, Joel, on
the other. The meeting had been delayed by the
grave illness of Pickering, who was Rhodes' best
friend and chief lieutenant. Rhodes nursed him to
the end and brought Dr. Jameson to his bedside.
But there was nothing to be done, and Pickering
gradually sunk into unconsciousness. When he died,
Rhodes, who had taken a great liking to Jameson,
decided to give the young and brilliant doctor
Pickering's job. From that day on he worked hand
in hand with Jameson. The two men had a great
affection for each other. Jameson admired Rhodes;
Rhodes trusted Jameson. " Jameson," said Rhodes,
" knows his mind and is not afraid to act. He may
go rather fast at times but, if it is a fault, it is a
good one."

An indissoluble friendship was to grow up between
the two men, so strong that, as we shall see, it
resisted all the buffetings of fortune. In Jameson
Rhodes had found his equal for force of personality,

but the doctor was far more impetuous and far less capable of controlling his impetuosity.

As for Barnato, though defeated, he remained a lifelong friend of Rhodes. It had taken some time and a great deal of eloquence to convince him that, in the trust deed, political ends should be considered. To Barnato, the object of the negotiation was the sale of diamonds and nothing else; to Rhodes, it meant a company so constituted that its profits could be employed for northern expansion and eventually benefit the British Commonwealth. They argued all night; at dawn Barnato yielded. " You can't resist Rhodes," he said, " he ties you up. . . . Some people have a fancy for one thing, some for another. You want the means to go north; well, I suppose we must give in to you, but it isn't business."

No hard feelings. It had been no more than a game between two wild beasts; a rough one but with claws well sheathed. No hatred was involved. Barnato had one unsatisfied desire—to be entertained at the Kimberley Club. Rhodes magnanimously gave a luncheon in his honour there. Then he asked Barnato to satisfy one of his own ambitions, which was to see a whole bucketful of diamonds. It was a shrewd way of flattering and appeasing his former rival by acknowledging that he retained a superiority of wealth. Barnato produced the glittering bucket and Rhodes plunged his arms into it ecstatically.

There is another version of this story. According to it, Rhodes was afraid that Barnato, with his huge stock of sorted diamonds, would flood the market and kill the price. So he went to see him one evening and telling him of his ambition, which only he could realise, suddenly swept the whole tableful of diamonds, whose sorting had taken months, into a bucket that was at hand. The sorting would have to be done all over again, and Rhodes had gained a breathing space. Both versions have their points.

Here then was Rhodes, aged thirty-five, and controlling ninety per cent of the world's diamond production; undisputed master of Goldfields of South Africa, which shortly brought him the enormous income of £400,000 per annum, and he had just been re-elected for Barkly West. Financially and politically he dominated South Africa. Through his immense wealth he could influence British policy, and even that of the United States. His object was to be a benevolent despot. He treated his employees well and gave them model housing conditions, but anyone who tried to take an independent line was pulverised. " Philanthropy is all very well in its way," he would say, " but philanthropy plus five per cent is a great deal better." Absolute power is a terrible test for a man, and few pass it with impunity. But in Rhodes's eyes it was the essential lever for building the continent of his dreams, the continent that was to be both imperial and free.

* 7 *

Northward Ho!

THE GRAND outline of Rhodes's imperial scheme
was to unite the red area in the north, the Sudan,
with the red in the south. In this connection no
territory was more important than the high plateau
to the north of the Transvaal, to which he had
secured an avenue of approach by the annexation
of Bechuanaland. He always referred to this area
as " My North," but in fact his north was inhabited
by a powerful native tribe, the Matabeles, whose
royal Kraal was at Bulawayo.

Matabele means the hidden people, and they were
so named because of the enormous ox-hide shields
behind which they hid in battle. The tribe was of
Zulu origin. On the Great Trek in 1837 the Boers
had driven the Matabeles before them and Moselikatze, their King, had retreated northwards from
the Transvaal and had established himself on the
rich pastures south of the Zambesi. The Matabeles
had defeated and " eaten up " the native tribes that

had occupied the land before them. The conquerors called the conquered people " *Mashonas*," a term of contempt. The remaining Mashonas were pushed into a territory which was called Mashonaland, and lay north-west of Matabeleland. Moselikatze died in 1868 and, after two years of civil war among the Matabeles, was succeeded, in 1870, by his son, Lo Bengula, who still reigned over Matabeleland and Mashonaland, at Bulawayo, in 1885.

Since the defeat of the Zulus in 1879, the Matabeles had been the only native armed force in South Africa. They were a militant and half-Spartan tribe, whose young males were brought up as warriors. Fed entirely on beef, the healthy became strong and fierce, the weaklings died of dysentery. They were forbidden to marry until they were twenty-five and had been blooded in battle. Their battle training was achieved by means of ecstatic war dances for which they wore a cape and head-dress of ostrich feathers, adorned their brows with a strip of otter skin, their legs with ox tails, and were attired in a kind of wild cat skin kilt. Instead of manœuvres they carried out real raids on their neighbours. Their king, Lo Bengula, who was more of a statesman and less of a soldier than his father, did not want war with the whites, but he claimed the right to refuse them access to his territories. As for the Boers, who saw themselves

shut in on east and west, the only remaining hope
was the north, and they sought Lo Bengula's permission to settle within his frontiers.

At Christmas time, in 1887, when Sir Hercules
Robinson, the Governor of the Cape and High
Commissioner for South Africa, was quietly preparing festivities to celebrate Queen Victoria's Golden
Jubilee, Rhodes descended on him like a tornado.
He had just learned that Kruger was on the point
of signing a treaty of friendship with Lo Bengula.
The treaty had not yet been ratified, but it would
constitute a terrible threat to Rhodes's empire-
building plans for the northern territories. It was
imperative to take action. Sir Hercules would have
been content to " wait and see," but no more than
Barney Barnato could he resist the force of Rhodes,
who deployed all his seductiveness, outlined the
dreams he had worked out in his mind, and, in the
end, overbore the Governor. As before, and as
always, it was impossible to refuse him anything.
The mixture of almost childish insistence with poetic
grandeur confounded all his critics.

" We have enough territory already," the
Governor interposed timidly.

" The builders of the original fortress on Table
Mountain said then, ' We have enough territory.'
And look where you are now! " answered Rhodes.

"And where," asked the Governor, "will you draw the line?"

Rhodes unrolled a map and pointed to the south of Tanganyika. So much ambition hinted at plenty of difficulties to come, and Sir Hercules sighed— but gave in. He started by giving Rhodes a free rein: "I will leave you alone," he said. But he ended up by supporting him.

There was at the time an Englishman called Moffat, a relation of Livingstone's, on a mission to Lo Bengula. Moffat was given instructions by the Government and implemented them to such effect that by 11 February 1888, the native ruler had been persuaded to sign a permanent treaty of friendship with Great Britain. Lo Bengula undertook to cede no territory and sign no treaty without the previous authority of the British High Commissioner.

To Rhodes it was an option; it only remained to acquire possession. Now, in the early days of 1888, he was all set for the adventure. "Goldfields" and "De Beers" were getting along perfectly well by themselves, so that he could give himself heart and soul to the problem of Matabeleland. He at once dispatched a mission to Bulawayo under his old friend Rudd, with Thompson, who had studied local dialects and customs since childhood, and Maguire, a Fellow of All Souls and one of the Twelve Apostles.

Rhodes still stuck to his preference for Oxford men.

Lo Bengula received the English courteously. He was a large, fat man, who went about naked apart from a blue cloth round his midriff and an apron of monkey skins hanging down like a sporan. Of clean and distinguished appearance, he held himself upright, thumping his chest and palavering politely. He was not badly disposed towards whites, but his bodyguard of young warriors would clearly have welcomed an opportunity to slaughter the Europeans, for all sorts of them kept turning up; Boer envoys, German traders, and missionaries. All Europeans were pestering Lo Bengula to obtain the right to mine the gold reefs in Mashonaland.

Rhodes's friends had a hard time persuading the Black King, who was surrounded by witch doctors and trusted them. If the Englishmen bathed, they were accused of bewitching the water. Yet, as Rhodes would have said, a witch doctor can generally be " squared " and Lo Bengula protected his guests well. At last, on 30 October 1888, the King, in his royal Kraal, was graciously pleased to grant Messrs. Rudd, Maguire and Thompson a concession of all the mining rights in his territory, including gold in Mashonaland, in token of which he affixed the elephant's seal on the concessionary document. The price was a monthly rent of £100, 1000 rifles, 100,000 rounds of ammunition and an armed steamer on the Zambesi. It was not dear. Rudd hurried off to bear Rhodes the precious treaty, but found all the watering places had dried up and almost died of thirst in the desert. He just had the strength to hide the contract in a great ant-eater's burrow before losing consciousness. He was fortunately discovered by friendly Bechuanas, who returned him to a British colony; he recovered the treaty and eventually brought it to Rhodes. It was now possible to found the British South Africa Company.

Though a great advance had been made, much remained to be done. Despite the protection of Lo Bengula, Thompson and Maguire, who had been held at Bulawayo, found themselves in some danger. Rival companies were being formed. Rhodes was always saying, "Nature abhors a vacuum." If he could not persuade the British Government to occupy Matabeleland, others, either Germans, Portuguese or Boers would do so. Already, Lo Bengula was dispensing concessions in a happy-go-lucky way to any white man who passed by. His mind was not very clear on the subject of under-takings and contracts. Rhodes had to buy off his rivals at fabulous prices, but this did not deter the great amalgamator.

His opponents at home caused him far greater concern than all the blacks or whites in Matabeleland. He hurried to London, determined to bring his vast wealth, his political contacts, his standing in the city and his charm into play. He would need all of them to succeed, for at the outset he was very badly received. The Society for the Protection of Aborigines criticised his methods and attacked him for paying the natives with arms; others accused him of making Kimberley a living hell, while others, still recalling his speech against " the Imperial factor," accused him of being an Afrikaner separatist or Home Ruler.

It took him six months to secure his charter. In the political world he had the support of the Cape Government and of Sir Hercules Robinson, who protested against " the amateur meddling of irresponsible and ill-advised persons in England." Rhodes secured the votes of the Irish Party in the House of Commons by giving Parnell £10,000 for his struggle for Home Rule. Provided the rights of Parliament were recognised, he thought that Irish Home Rule would mark out the way for Imperial Home Rule. As to the new territories he pointed out to the Colonial Office that administration by an independent company would effect a great economy for Her Majesty's Government. He won his game when he succeeded in persuading the Duke of Abercorn, the Duke of Fife, who was related to the Prince of Wales, and George Grey, who was known as " the paladin of his generation " (Parsifal led astray into a game of poker), to serve as directors on the Board of the new company. With such guarantors the game was won.

On 29 October 1889 the Queen-Empress graciously considered the humble petition presented to her by the Duke of Abercorn, President of the British South Africa Company, whose activities were to be concentrated in an area north of Bechuanaland and west of the Portuguese colonies. It is worth noticing that Rhodes had taken the precaution of not tying himself to frontiers in other directions. The petition declared that the petitioners would serve the interests of England, would promote commerce, civilisation and good government, would regulate the traffic in alcohol and suppress that in slaves; and that the achievement of these worthy aims would be facilitated if Her Majesty would see fit to grant the Company a Royal Charter of Incorporation. The Government were not loath to leave the initiative in Africa, which international competition made so inflammable, to an independent company which could be disowned if it failed. The Charter was granted and the Company known thenceforward by the shorter title " Chartered." The necessary capital had been subscribed with eagerness. How could the miracle worker in gold and diamonds, supported by the noble Dukes, fail to inspire confidence?

There were a million £1 shares: De Beers subscribed at once 200,000 of these. Goldfields and
Rhodes himself gave powerful support. Many
subscribers were found outside England. Never in
the nineteenth century had such gigantic power been
granted to a private company. The Charter might
be revoked if the Company misused its privileges,
but otherwise there was hardly anything they could
not do. They were given the right " to make
treaties, promulgate laws, preserve the peace,
maintain a police force and acquire new concessions."
The Times wrote: " Whether the Company finds
the wealth of Ophir in the mountains and rivers of
Mashonaland or not, we cannot doubt that it will
lay the basis of a great English-speaking colony in
what appear to be the fairest regions in Africa. . . ."
Chartered was not purely a trading company;
it was a sovereign state, subject only to distant
supervision by the British Government.

Rhodes had already left for South Africa, having
ordered two hundred and fifty miles of telegraph
wire for a line between Mafeking and Bulawayo.
The railway lines were to follow—" The railway
is my right hand and the telegraph my voice." The
Charter established Rhodes as the ruler of an area
as large as Germany and France put together. It
was something of a revelation to see a whole slice
of a continent being thus brought to life. In this

venture the pound sterling had played a rôle
normally assigned to rifle and cannon. But would
the Charter give him the power to exploit his initial
advantage? That was the great problem now
confronting Rhodes.

* 8 *

A Private Empire

ONCE MORE the admirable Dr. Jameson made the journey to Bulawayo to tell Lo Bengula of the formation of " Chartered." He was an old friend of the King's, for he had relieved him of gout on an earlier visit. This time he was accompanied by a mission from the Great White Queen, including a military band and the three tallest Life Guards. These giants were a great help in appeasing the black monarch, who was dismayed at finding he had given away more than he intended. He had granted a concession of mineral rights and here he was being told of an immigration which looked for all the world like an invasion. He felt tricked and would have liked to have it out with Rhodes himself, whom he called the Great White King. " I thought you had come to look for gold," he informed the Colonial Office, " but you also want to take my people from me." The Colonial Office, who had been pushed farther than they wished by Rhodes, explained the matter away to the Matabeles and echoed Jameson, who, in his reports, referred to the people whose dominions were being invaded as rebels. It should be added that Lo Bengula weathered these tests of his loyalty in a remarkable way; no emissary to whom he had given his protection was ever molested and as long as he reigned he showed a truly royal sense of hospitality. But his kingdom was no less in danger for this.

His only chance was that Rhodes had chosen to send his pioneers to Mashonaland rather than Matabeleland. In a way, it came to the same thing, as the Mashonas were tributaries of the Matabeles. Yet, if there was to be an argument, Rhodes preferred to argue with the unwarlike Mashonas. " Mashonaland was really a No Man's Land, a raiding ground for the Matabeles, a kind of reserve in which they went hunting when they wanted sport and loot in the form of girls, cattle and slave boys for herders. Since this North was unsurveyed, even unexplored, there could be no actual boundaries." An ideal playground for men like Rhodes, Rudd and Jameson.

At Kimberley Rhodes was trying to organise a column of pioneers to take over the concession territory. It was a question of moving about two hundred pioneers, with their provisions and baggage, over seven hundred miles of completely wild country.

Lo Bengula had promised safe passage for the pioneers, though with much reluctance. Thanks to Dr. Jameson, he seemed to accept the idea of white men occupying Mashonaland, but his young men were less resigned and threatened to stop any foreign " *impi* [raids]." An escort of one thousand two hundred men was suggested to Rhodes, but the Company could not shoulder such an expense. Meanwhile, at the Kimberley Club, Rhodes met a young man of twenty-three called Johnson who had just returned from a seven-month trek and had met Lo Bengula. He was prepared to guarantee the safety of the column with two hundred and fifty men. " Everybody tells me you are a lunatic," said Rhodes, " but I have an intuition that you are right and can do it." After all, he had himself shouldered huge responsibility at an early age. He entrusted the expedition to Johnson.

Which was the best route to take? Rhodes consulted the famous lion-hunter, Frederick Selous, who had twenty years' knowledge of Matabeleland. It was he who, ten years before, had broken to him the news of Herbert's death. His advice was to follow the Transvaal border as far as Tuli. Meanwhile Jameson, never lacking in courage, went to remind the King of his promise to grant the pioneers a free passage. This time he was not received in the Royal Kraal and only caught a glimpse of the

King, worried and preoccupied, turning in small circles in the shadows of a mud hut. Jameson returned without his answer, but all Lo Bengula's original promises were destined to be scrupulously observed. " The King never lies," said the black monarch.

At the beginning of May 1890 the first Chartered pioneers, one hundred and eighty-four strong, mustered at Mafeking. Rhodes himself had collected mounts for them. Selous had recruited a force of two hundred natives who would push on ahead and clear the way for the road-makers. On 27 June the column set off. It was made up of ninety wagons and a mobile sawmill. Selous had plotted a safe route as far as Tuli. But from there onwards they crossed over swampy marshland and through thick scrub, ideal for an ambush, until on 18 August, having come to no harm, they climbed a steep gorge, which they christened Providential Pass, and came out on the open plains of Mashonaland. A powerful searchlight they had as part of their equipment had terrified the Matabele warriors. (The magic eye of white man.) On 11 September they reached their objective, a point which they called Fort Salisbury, without loss. They had done good work, marking out a road, building forts and establishing stages for a postal service.

Rhodes had not been able to go with the column,

having just become Prime Minister of the Cape,
thanks to Dutch support. He had done everything
in his power to reassure the Dutch, and in particular
had insisted that Boers, as much as Englishmen,
should be allowed to join Chartered's first pioneers.
A message was sent on the column's arrival at Fort
Salisbury and it came as a great relief to him:
" When at last I discovered they were through, I
do not think there was a happier man in the country
than myself."

At the end of October, he went, with two Dutch
members of Parliament for Cape Town, to in-
augurate the first stretch of the railway. On his
way he went through Pretoria to see Kruger and
to satisfy himself that the Boers were not going to
encroach on the concession, and to promise them
in exchange large farms on his land. Besides, he
needed farmers badly, for the supply of foodstuffs in
the new territories was very poor and dreadfully
expensive. Chartered's first year was described by
a pioneer to Rhodes himself as " a bloody fiasco."
Its credit in London was waning. The complaints
of the pioneers filtered through to the City; the
failure to find gold in any paying quantities painfully
surprised the shareholders; the cost of administration during the first year ran up to £250,000, owing
to the need for keeping up a police force of seven
hundred. The directors at home sent Rhodes frantic

requests for better news and mining discoveries. The £1 shares, which had been at a huge premium, fell below par. Rhodes decided to send his " trouble-shooter-in-chief," Jameson, on a tour of inspection, and the doctor made some severe cuts in the far too extravagant administration. He reduced the police force from 700 to 100 by persuading the colonists to volunteer. Then Rhodes arrived in person and in two months regained the confidence of all his followers. He conciliated the natives, listened to the grievances of the pioneers and communicated to everyone his optimism and energy.

Northward Ho! He was now dreaming of reaching the great lakes, of linking up with the Sudan and establishing a belt of British territory along which a Cape to Cairo railway could be built. He therefore planted a foot in Nyasaland, where there had been Scottish missionaries ever since the death of Livingstone. With some brave and fierce-looking Sikhs, imported from India, he organised a police force there and supported them with two armed steamers on Lake Nyasa and Lake Tanganyika. He established British law and later Chartered took over the whole administration of the territory. Meanwhile, other countries, such as Belgium, Portugal and Germany, were displaying grave anxiety over so much annexation.

As early as 1890 he had had to treat with Germany

and Belgium, who surrounded the great lakes on the east and west. But all that he had then asked for was a passage between Lake Nyasa and Lake Tanganyika, known as the Stevenson Road, to ensure contact with the north. By means of sentimental arguments he had persuaded the British Government to hold firm on this point. On this particular corridor stood the tree under which Livingstone had died; but what was more Rhodes had cunningly christened two forts on it Fort Fife and Fort Abercorn: " I knew they would not give up a fort named after a member of the Royal Family." In 1891 a treaty with Portugal, whose territories, Angola and Mozambique, were adjacent to the Chartered empire, enabled him to acquire further vast areas and to open the Portuguese port, Beira, to the Company's commerce. A railway was to be built between Beira and Salisbury, which would bring the mining centre to within 380 miles of the coast instead of the 2000 mile journey to Cape Town.

These negotiations, and the frontiers laid down by them, were more than satisfactory. Rhodes was becoming master of an autonomous and uncontested empire. But at the heart of the empire things were not going so well. Lo Bengula, becoming progressively more dissatisfied, was seeing his worst fears confirmed. He thought he had only ceded the right to exploit the subsoil, but Chartered was behaving as though it owned the land itself. The Mashonas, Lo Bengula's subjects and tributaries, were living among the colonists. How was their allegiance to be determined? The younger warriors of the Matabele King determined it in their own fashion by raiding and pillaging the intruders as well as the ever-suffering Mashonas, who, feeling unprotected, lost their respect for the white man. The colonists did not feel safe; they envied the King his fine grazing and fat herds; before long they coveted them. "Until Lo Bengula is crushed," the settlers said, "the success of the country either as a mining concern, or a new market and administration, will never be accomplished."

In 1893 Lo Bengula's "Young Bloods" carried out a particularly extensive raid. The colonists notified Jameson, who had now become their Governor, and he decided to dispatch a punitive expedition. Rhodes sent him a note: "Have you read Luke xiv, 31?" This is the text which reads: "Or what king, going to make war against another king, sitteth not down first, and consulteth whether he be able with ten thousand to meet him that cometh against him with twenty thousand." Jameson replied that he had read it, had sat down and consulted and that all would be well. Three months elapsed before hostilities began. Rhodes prepared for war, bought horses, enrolled men and sold 40,000 Chartered shares at a loss to cover expenses. He felt that, if there was to be a disaster, he was the person who had to bear the burden. The " volunteers " required Jameson to sign an agreement by which every man who fought the Matabeles was to receive a farm of six thousand acres and twenty gold claims. After that, war seemed inevitable. The settlers had said they would " either do something to bring a row or leave the country." Jameson sent an ultimatum to the Matabeles, who were collected round Victoria carrying their guns and spears, and gave them an hour in which to be gone.

They were obeying the order when a single rifle shot was fired and a man fell dead. Then Sir Henry Loch, who represented Her Majesty's Government in the negotiations with Lo Bengula, gave Jameson permission to start. Jameson, a Jack of all trades, and as good a soldier as he was a doctor, pushed on towards Bulawayo. It was a short, easy and successful campaign. He routed the warriors with the ox-hide shields and seized the Royal Kraal, to which Lo Bengula had set fire before fleeing. This unfortunate ruler died of small-pox a few months later. He was a man of good faith, who, even in the heat of battle, had protected four European negotiators who were living at his court. The Europeans did not do half as well by him, and a message for Rhodes, which he had entrusted to a soldier, was never delivered. Yet Jameson had meant to be magnanimous towards his royal patient and had sent a note to the fugitive: " To stop this useless slaughter, you must at once come to see me at Bulawayo, where I guarantee your life will be safe and that you will be kindly treated. I sign myself your former and, I hope, your present friend: L. S. JAMESON." But there again there was treachery and the letter was translated to the King by a bad man who told him: " It's a trap." So Lo Bengula never came. Rhodes suffered some remorse on account of this sad, black ghost and, at a later date, undertook the education of Lo Bengula's three sons.

Lo Bengula's defeat rendered the Company absolute ruler of all the Matabele territories apart from a native reserve. By the same token it seized all the cattle in the country apart from a few which were left to the natives for milk. In short Rhodes was in complete control of everything between Bechuanaland and the Zambesi. At the end of 1894 Jameson, or " Doctor Jim " as his admirers called him, returned to London and was fêted all round.

Back in England Chartered had a wonderful press. At the Company's annual meeting in 1892 Rhodes had been present, had heard the noble Dukes sing his praises and had been wildly applauded by his shareholders. It was true that Chartered shares did not pay a dividend, but they could be sold at a premium and they gave their holders rights in profitable ventures such as South African railways. Moreover the shareholders considered it an honour to support this great enterprise. The British South Africa Chartered Company was more imperial than commercial.

He had described the march of more than 1000 miles into totally unexplored country; he had eulogised Jameson, his gallant companion, who, on a single word from him, and regardless of a high fever, had travelled 690 miles to take up his post; he had explained why he had been determined not to delay the occupation of the territory north of the Zambesi; " I didn't think it right to take two bites at a cherry." From first to last the speech was delivered in his familiar manner, unaffected and humorous. But was he joking when he said, " I am on the best of terms with President Kruger," or did he really think he was?

The Queen received him to luncheon, and he was amazed to discover how well informed she was about the future prospects in Mashonaland and else-where. She made him expatiate on the Kimberley mines and the treatment of diamonds. He outlined to her his grandiose plans for enlarging the empire: in 1894 he was able to report that, since his previous

audience with her, he had added 12,000 square
miles to her dominions; and, he said, the Transvaal,
" which we should never have given up," would one
day return to the Crown. The Queen was delighted:
she described him as " a tremendously strong man."
When one of her ladies-in-waiting objected that
he was said to be a woman-hater she protested,
" Oh! But he was extremely kind to me! " That
was undeniable, and Rhodes always remained in
the good graces of his sovereign.

The annual meeting of 1895 was one long hymn
of triumph. The Company had passed through all
its military trials. The valour of a band of heroes
had assured England of mammoth lands without a
single penny's expense being borne by the taxpayer.
The ferocity of a band of natives had constrained
Jameson to impose the Pax Britannica on the
Matabeles. The Duke of Fife moved a vote of
thanks to Mr. Cecil Rhodes, whose name was
already pledged to posterity as one who had built
a " greater Britain." In his reply Rhodes spoke of
the good relations he retained with his neighbours.
He admired the Portuguese, for had not Henry the
Navigator English blood in his veins? There was
no sort of difficulty with the Transvaal. " Your sole
purpose," he told his English friends and colleagues,
" should be to expand your commerce. You are not,
like the French, farmers of wide acres; you are a

small kingdom which produces primary products and distributes them the whole world over. The concern of each one of you is with the four corners of the earth; your life is not England merely, but the world."

In this same year of '95 Chartered raised fresh capital, which was heavily over-subscribed in London and Paris. The one pound shares now stood at nine pounds; the Company's railways were advancing; its ports opening their arms. All was well with the world.

* 9 *

At the Top of the
Greasy Pole

So, at the age of forty-two, Rhodes reached the top of the greasy pole. The Queen had made him a Privy Councillor, so that he was now the Rt. Hon. Cecil Rhodes; the Postmaster-General's office had approved the name Rhodesia as describing the Chartered Company's territories—Southern Rhodesia and Northern Rhodesia were soon to be shown in every atlas. " Well, you know, to have a bit of country named after one is one of the things a man might be proud of."

In Rhodesia he ruled over 750,000 square miles. Three years after its occupation by Jameson Bulawayo had become a fine city complete with hotels, newspapers and telegraph offices. The civic offices had appropriately been built on the spot where the hapless Lo Bengula used to administer justice from under his tree. From Mafeking and Beira railways were spreading out towards Salisbury. Farming flourished, the gold mines were progressing and the colonists were gaining in confidence.

At the Cape Rhodes was practically unopposed as Prime Minister. He overcame his opponents in conversations outside the House. " Sit down and argue with a man," he used to urge. But his arguments were not always on an intellectual plane. His old dictum, "Can't you square him?" continued to carry weight. His great ambition was still to be " the Great Amalgamator." Not only was he determined to unite South Africa, but he also wanted to bring her into closer touch with other members of the Empire. He used some of the Cape's financial reserves to help Australia through a crisis in 1893 and he sent Cape representatives to Canada to settle tariff questions between the two countries.

He also occupied himself with numerous internal problems. He established a Ministry of Agriculture which, by introducing the American coccinella, saved the orange groves from destruction by insects. He had the French methods of countering phylloxera investigated and revived the vineyards by importing young vines from America. He brought over Arab stallions to improve the existing strain and, from the Sultan of Morocco, he procured Angora goats to cross with the local breed. In spite of opposition, he passed a " Scab Act " by which flocks of sheep infected with scabies could be isolated. In short, action, and effective action at that, was being taken everywhere.

He would have liked to reform the Cape University, by uniting the English and Boer colleges, but here he failed. The prejudices involved were too strong even for him. Conflicting interests can always be reconciled—passions never. But at least he did everything possible to recall the original Dutch colonisation, by setting up statues of the founders and by having all the old records classified. The object of his native policy was the same—unity of method. " I hope we shall have *one* native policy in South Africa." At this time he favoured segregation of the less civilised natives, who would only otherwise imitate the shortcomings of the whites, but by the end of his life he had taken up a position which could be summed up by the formula: " Equal rights for all civilised men south of the Zambesi." He was opposed to slavery, and hoped the natives would acquire self-respect, but insisted on their doing an honest day's work. He had a strong aversion for " loafers," whatever their colour.

He was, in fact, very popular with the natives, who called him " The Father of the People." If they felt injured on any score they would say among themselves, " wait till the Old Man comes." Black or White, whoever had a complaint could bring it to him. These visitors seldom came for disinterested reasons, but he knew it and always began the conversation himself with: " What do you want? " He always came to the rescue of those in trouble or of young people who had ideas but lacked capital. Some of them he knew were not honest, but ever since he had refused help to one man who had then killed himself, he preferred to risk being fleeced rather than be the cause of despair.

He was a fabulously rich man who had few personal wants. Dressed like a tramp, he lived, in many ways, like a student. His manservant, Tony, bought him white flannel trousers, strange buttoned boots and blue ties with white spots by the dozen. But in no time the trousers were all creased and his clothes covered with stains. On one occasion when, as Prime Minister, he was going to open an exhibition in Cape Town, one of the doorkeepers turned him away. Another time at Salisbury he sent a dirty old overcoat with a hole burnt in it, but with which he did not wish to part, to a cleaner to be cleaned and mended. It was returned to him with a note which read, " Dear Sir, Herewith the Right Honourable Cecil Rhodes's coat uncleaned and unmended. We regret that all we can do with the garment is to make a new coat to match the buttons."

For a long time he had had no home; at the Cape he lived in a hotel and at Kimberley in Jameson's cottage. But as Prime Minister he had to entertain and needed a house in Cape Town. In 1893 he bought an old warehouse at the foot of Table Mountain, which had belonged to the Netherlands East India Company. It was called De Groote Schuur or the Great Barn. He kept the Dutch name, for political reasons, and engaged a young architect, Herbert Baker, to restore it. In the course of his travels in South Africa Herbert Baker had discovered the beauty of the old Dutch farms, which were far better suited to the climate and conditions than were the fantasies of contemporary designers.

" I want the big and simple, barbaric if you like," Rhodes told him, and Baker went back to the original plan and rebuilt in dignified Dutch colonial style: a thatched roof, teak ceilings and panelling (a whole boatload of wood was used) and Netherlands furniture, bought from outlying farms or copied by local carpenters in local materials. There was little bric-à-brac: Old Dutch crystal lustres, china from Delft or India, and archaic gold objects found in Mashonaland, where a long-extinct race had had a genius for engraving gold sun-dials and for carving birds in soapstone. It is a strange thing to see how this great English adventurer wanted to link himself to the Dutch, or even pre-historic, origins of the country he had recreated.[1]

There were no pictures on the walls: he thought

[1] Basil Williams, p.220.

they were too expensive: " Why, if I had a twenty thousand pound picture hanging there, the pleasure from looking at it would be spoilt because I would feel: ' There's two miles of my Cape to Cairo railway hanging on my wall.' " Instead, he had an excellent library: The classics, travel and a collection of Gibbon's sources, for which he had Europe scoured. It had cost him a fortune and was never any use to him or to anyone else. The whim of an erudite millionaire with a strong and individual will. Everything in the house belonged to a particular style, from the drawing-room walls adorned with Spanish embossed leather to the copper spittoons and kitchen utensils. Rhodes was specially attached to a small oak table engraved by the children of the royal family, which the Queen had given him.

But he was chiefly proud of the magnificent view towards the mountain from his bedroom window, of the huge park full of rare trees and giant flowers in which he had set up a reserve for big game: antelopes, zebras, ostriches and even a few lions in cages. At the foot of Table Mountain he made a great avenue of pines—" I love to think that human beings will walk that road long after I am gone." He had a passion for creating beauty and his religion was primarily natural. He had tried to introduce singing birds from Europe; in their new surroundings they continued to live but no longer sang. The squirrels he imported flourished to the extent of becoming a pest.

This park was open to everyone. In its glades strollers could sit on teak benches as they would in public gardens ; some even came on to the veranda and ordered tea. In the pine wood at the foot of the mountain was a small cottage, the Woolsack, where Rudyard Kipling spent several winters, writing, towards the end of Rhodes's life. Kipling, the poet of Empire, must have been intrigued by Rhodes, the poet of action. He found him as inarticulate as a fifteen-year-old schoolboy. Rhodes still had a way of asking brusque, naïve questions, which were as disconcerting as a child's— or, alternatively, as a Roman Emperor's, which was very much what Rhodes was like—a Roman Emperor with a moustache. Of Kipling he demanded, " What is your dream? " Having lived for his own he imagined everyone else did the same.

From the park you could climb to the top of the mountain up a lovely ravine, full of blue hydrangeas. Ferns and moss lined the banks of the stream, and Rhodes often went as far as an inconspicuous ledge, from which he could see the two oceans, " to be alone with the Alone." There, as in Rhodesia, he enjoyed his only great delight, a sense of creation —for this park and this view were his creation.

He got up early every day and went for a walk,

taking with him files which he scrutinised and then left behind at points where he had dismounted. He ran through the newspapers rapidly during break-fast, and then went to the Chartered offices in Cape Town. There he indulged in his favourite pastime of astonishing his colleagues with feats of memory. He was intolerant and would sack any he found slow-witted, and then, overcome by remorse, call them back and, circling round them with an embarrassed air, end up by blurting: " Do you want any money? " He went home for lunch and then read, again leaving his books and papers about in the most unexpected places. At five o'clock he had strong, black tea. Then followed the signing of official papers and dinner. After dinner he either immersed himself in grandiose schemes for the future or else played a very bad game of billiards or bridge. Occasionally he entertained old friends from Kimberley or Johannesburg, some Boer farmer or a political colleague. At eleven o'clock he went to bed.

But his great joy was to set off on trek over the veld, as in the old days. He travelled slowly with a wagonette for himself and his companion, another for his valet, Tony, and the provisions, and some horses to ride. He bought anything he wanted on the way, " to encourage commerce." The gun pro-vided fresh meat. A tub of warm water and a large sponge were all that was needed for washing. He liked to be on trek from morning to evening, only pausing for meals. He was as intrigued with every incident of the journey as he had been on his first trek at the age of eighteen. Having no sense of direction, he was always afraid of getting lost on the veld and would never be left alone. To stand next to him when he was shooting was to stand in mortal danger.

On these treks he always took a Plutarch, Bryce's American Commonwealth, a volume of Plato's Dialogues and a pocket edition of Marcus Aurelius. The Emperor's philosophic reflections were very valuable to him: " Consider the whole of nature, of which you are such a small part; and the whole of time, to which you have been assigned but a fleeting moment; and destiny, of which you are the barest particle." Very healthy thoughts for a man who was too powerful. " When things around you give cause for alarm, return to your own pace at once and do not depart from it more than necessity ordains." The silence of the veld brought Rhodes back to a slower and wiser pace. On these occasions he indulged his two passions: to meditate and to be alone with Nature.

But while he was yet at the height of his triumph the first signs of a hostile destiny began to appear. Following a serious bout of influenza he had some worrying and painful heart attacks. It now occurred to him that he might not live to a great age. For this reason he wanted to race death, to complete his grand design before death put an end to everything for him. At such moments Marcus Aurelius was forgotten. Rhodes, as impassioned and impatient as ever, was no longer in full control of himself. There was every reason to fear the worst.

* 10 *

The Jameson Raid

THE HIGHER Rhodes stood above other men the fewer potential opponents could he see before him. His only remaining antagonist of any significance in 1895 was the ageing President of the Transvaal, Paul Kruger. Not that Rhodes either thought himself, or wished to be, the enemy of the Afrikaners. On the contrary it had long been his policy to conciliate them and look to them for support. He thought he had united the Boers and the English for their common good in South Africa. But he regarded South Africa as a federation under the British flag, while Kruger, savagely jealous of his country's independence, remained the champion of the Great Trek towards liberty.

The pious Kruger saw Rhodes as no better than a bare-faced financier and the Devil incarnate. Was it not he with his gold and diamonds who had attracted so many greedy foreigners to the country that they now outnumbered the Boers themselves.

And yet in his way Rhodes was an idealist. Rather than a financier he would have preferred to be a messiah, the prophet of Anglo-Saxon dominion. " Do you think that any part of Africa was left in perpetuity for the pigmies while a superior race stands multiplying outside? I do not believe it. Our race will never adopt the doctrines of Malthus. They will go on multiplying and probably in 200 years, they will fill the whole world."

Here were two fanatics standing face to face and no good was likely to come of it. The main bone of contention between them was the status of foreigners in the Transvaal. Kruger, who was afraid of being submerged by them, refused them political rights, the right to naturalisation as well as the right to vote. The " Uitlanders," who were mostly English, retaliated, on the occasion of a visit from members of the Cape Government, by replacing the Boer flag with the English one. Besides, by imposing excessive import duties on English goods, Kruger was putting up the cost of living; he favoured the building of the Portuguese railway at the expense of the British one, and he created monopolies for the sale of dynamite and cyanide, which were essential to the miners. Even more serious, the old Boer, who was of German origin, would, from time to time, wave the menace of German intervention. To some Boer citizens, who nevertheless thought some of the foreigners' complaints well-founded and echoed them, Kruger simply replied, " Go back and tell your people that I shall never give them anything. I shall never change my policy. And now let the storm burst." A compromise would have suited all parties far better, but Kruger was a man of " character," and as Clemenceau used to say, " when one has character it is always bad."

In short Kruger was standing in Rhodes's way and Rhodes would not tolerate it. From time to time he went to Johannesburg, which was the mining centre for the foreigners, whereas Pretoria was the Boer capital, and there he and Jameson listened to the grievances of the " Uitlanders," who were beginning to talk of revolt. An organised body of " Reformers " had grown up among them and they were appealing for a union of capitalists and workers against the Boers. In truth the workers were not very enthusiastic and many of the capitalists, those who were not English, distrusted all armed intervention and preferred to stick to their methods of bargaining and bribes, which had served well enough so far. But Rhodes, under-estimating the strength of the Boers, aware of his illness and anxious to complete his task in his lifetime, was girding his loins for action.

He thought his success as assured as it had been against Lo Bengula. He imagined that Joseph Chamberlain and the Colonial Office would give him official support. The Colonial Office had already allowed him a strip of land along the Transvaal frontier for his railway, and the right to police it, which enabled him to set up armed guards against attack. At Bulawayo Jameson was forming a body of volunteers. One of Rhodes's men was buying arms in England and the Government was taking no notice, which encouraged him to think he was being authorised to start a revolt. The idea of armed intervention appealed to him more and more, although he was Prime Minister of a country on good terms with the Transvaal. Too much power and success will blind even the most intelligent men.

In the Transvaal the " Reformers " were receiving their contraband arms, but they sensed the hesitancy of their troops. At Johannesburg many moderates were trying to keep out of the conspiracy. But it was deepening and the messages pouring into the Chartered offices at Cape Town were reminiscent of a second-rate detective story. The plot was called " the polo tournament," the conspirators " the shareholders." Jameson was to lead an army of liberation and he had sent out a forerunner to prepare stage posts for horses and provisions between the frontier and Johannesburg. The revolt at Johannesburg was to coincide with the Christmas rush. Kruger was well informed of all these preparations and allowed them to go ahead. " If you want to kill a tortoise," he said, " you must wait until it puts out its head, and then you cut it off."

But the nearer the great day approached the more uneasy the conspirators in Johannesburg became. It was obvious that the plot was an open secret. Many miners and traders had already sent their wives and children away and there was no more room on the trains for Cape Town although the services had been doubled and even trebled. On 27 December 1895 the Reformers' Committee published a manifesto declaring that the National Union, the name they had given their movement, had resolved to secure equal rights, genuine parliamentary government, freedom of exchange in all South Africa and equality for the Dutch and English languages. " There's what we want. How shall we secure it? " asked Leonard, the President of the Union, whose base was the headquarters of Goldfields of South Africa—a sufficient proof of Rhodes's connivance.

Young men in high yellow boots and sombreros galloped about the streets of Johannesburg, but they were not well armed, and the miners and traders seemed to be hostile. Jameson had only been able to collect seven hundred volunteers instead of the anticipated fifteen hundred. Even the Reformers asked for the operation to be postponed. Rhodes's comment on the situation was: "The thing has fizzled out like a damp squib." But on the frontier Jameson was champing at the bit. He also was a sick man, a slightly bowed figure with an anxious expression, although his famous smile still lit up his face from time to time. He could hide his impatience, but had an ungovernable thirst for movement, danger and adventure.

He convinced himself that if the raid was postponed his men would disband, while the Boers would mobilise. Besides, everything had gone right for him up till now; he had faith in his lucky star; he believed that if he confronted the British Government, Rhodes and his Johannesburg friends with an accomplished fact they would all be obliged to follow him, and having triumphed he would be forgiven. It was in vain that on the 28th the Reformers dispatched two envoys to dissuade him. His answer was, "I'm going in," and on Sunday the 29th at 21.30 hours he launched his raid. He notified Rhodes by telegraph, but the reply ordering him not to move never reached Jameson, for the wires had been cut. Kipling, who had a taste for the supernatural, maintained that Rhodes and

Jameson communicated by telepathy, but that this time the system broke down.

At Johannesburg Jameson was awaited hourly. The cynics murmured: " After all, the Boers know all about raising a commando, and how to fight; they could quite easily halt the raid." " Not at all," answered the supporters of the Union, " the Boers are not what they used to be, and besides, we have bought off their leaders." But this was wishful thinking. As it turned out, Boers streamed into Pretoria, with cartridge cases slung over their shoulders and their old felt hats on their heads. In some parties three generations of the same family could be identified. Four days after the invasion, Kruger controlled 5,000 armed men.

But it was all over already. Jameson had advanced by forced marches as far as Krugersdorp where the Boers began to harass him on the flanks and from the rear in their guerrilla fashion. On January 1st the invaders still retained numerical superiority, but by the following day, at Doornkop, the Boers had been reinforced and Jameson, driven into a valley, saw his men encircled and sniped at by the wonderfully accurate fire of the Burghers, who remained invisible and invulnerable behind boulders on the kopjes. " We were fighting against puffs of smoke," one of the officers explained. With sixty-five killed and thirty-seven wounded, and unable to retaliate, Jameson, who had fought bravely while hope lasted, was forced to hoist the white flag. Then the Boers came running down from the hills like madmen to take the survivors, Jameson included, prisoner. They were shepherded to Pretoria and there imprisoned.

* 11 *

The Aftermath

THE DAY before the fateful decision, Rhodes was sitting calmly at Groote Schuur, for he imagined his telegram had stopped Jameson. But in the evening he learned that the wires had been cut and immediately realised the catastrophic nature of the situation. He told Sir Graham Bower: "I know I shall have to go: I shall resign to-morrow." The following day he remained unseen, wandering by himself on Table Mountain. He did not want to do anything that might compromise Jameson's chances. At last, in the evening, he received a visitor, who found him, for the first time in his life, in a state of collapse: "Yes, yes, it is true, it is all true! Old Jameson has upset my apple-cart."

"Why don't you stop him?"

"Poor old Jameson! Twenty years we have been friends and now he goes and ruins me. I cannot go and destroy him."

This was before he knew the worst.

Rejected and blamed by everyone, he handed in his resignation, but refused to publish a word disowning Jameson.

" Well, you see, Jameson has been such an old friend. Of course I cannot do it."

For Rhodes, so accustomed to success, they were terrible days. His valet, Tony, recounted how he stayed up for eight days and nights. His heart disease was certainly aggravated. He could see no way out of the situation and no end to his downfall. He suddenly lost faith in the Cape Dutch, his political supporters, and it became clear that he would never again be the leader of the South African community. His brother Frank, and all his best friends, as well as Jameson, were in prison at Pretoria and under shadow of the death sentence.

The British Government had no choice but to disown Rhodes and Jameson. In some countries it is still firmly held that Chamberlain knew all about Rhodes's plans, but that this was never revealed because Rhodes refused to compromise Her Majesty's Government. But since all the evidence has been destroyed the truth of the matter will never be known. At Johannesburg a deep gloom had replaced the drilling of gaily-coloured horsemen. The Governor of the Cape, Sir Hercules Robinson, had immediately left for Pretoria. On his way across the Orange Free State he had seen a small army preparing to go to the rescue of the sister republic.

In England, public opinion had at first been against Rhodes, but was completely reversed by news of a telegram sent to Kruger by Kaiser William II, congratulating him on having defeated the invaders without even calling upon friendly powers for help. It was tantamount to saying that Germany was only too ready to intervene. This was already suspected, but the clumsy and ill-timed demonstration of it succeeded in reviving Rhodes's popularity. Neither the English nor the Dutch had any wish to be invaded by Germany on the pretext of helping the Boers. The leader of the Afrikaner party in the Cape, Hofmeyer, was seized with unholy rage when he heard of the Kaiser's telegram. " No one knows better than His Imperial Majesty," he said, " that the first shot fired by Germany against England would be immediately followed by the seizure of all the German colonies by the British fleet." At a later date Rhodes explained to the Kaiser:

" You see, I was a naughty boy and you tried to whip me. Now *my* people were quite ready to whip me for being a naughty boy, but directly *you* did it, they said: ' No, if this is anybody's business, it is *ours*.' The result was that Your Majesty got yourself very much disliked by the English people, and I never got whipped at all."

From all over South Africa telegrams poured in to the High Commissioner begging him to save Jameson, who had been sentenced to death by a Boer court martial. Sir Hercules Robinson intervened in Johannesburg to secure the surrender of all their arms by the conspirators, and in Pretoria to persuade Kruger to pass a more lenient sentence. The High Commissioner very probably supported his action with irresistible arguments. The " tragicomedy of errors " ended with little loss of blood once the fighting was over. Jameson was handed over to the British Government for trial in London. He was sentenced to eighteen months' imprisonment under the Foreign Enlistment Act, but was released after a year on grounds of ill-health and returned to Rhodesia, where he was still very popular.

As for the ringleaders in Johannesburg, the signatories of the appeal to Jameson (the Reformers), they were sentenced to death, but, in face of protests by the Burghers themselves, Kruger set them free on payment of a fine of £25,000, most of which came out of Rhodes's pocket.

The expenses of the raid, the arms and pay, were shared between Rhodes and Beit. All the participants of the dreadful blunder got off lightly except Rhodes, who had to resign from all his posts including the Board of Chartered, the company of his creation. Did he suffer an injustice? It is true that he had knowledge of, and had given previous approval to, Jameson's plans; that, with extraordinary lack of scruple he had encouraged this private invasion which was to be made without a declaration of war; but he had also, at the critical moment, tried to restrain Jameson, and it is possible that others, higher placed than he, had had an undivulged responsibility. It is to Rhodes's great credit that he made use of neither of these arguments, that he covered his superiors and his subordinates, and conducted himself magnificently throughout the whole lamentable affair. The training of Marcus Aurelius had had its effect.

At the beginning of 1896 he made a short visit to London to assure himself that nothing was threatening the position of Chartered itself, but returned at once when a serious crisis developed among the Matabeles. The Jameson raid had denuded their territory of its police force; epizootic disease was ravaging their herds, and turning their grazing reserves into graveyards; worst of all they were losing confidence in the whites, who were fighting among themselves. Rhodes felt his presence was essential. He came back by way of Egypt so as to consult Kitchener, who for his part was advancing through the Sudan towards the great lakes, and whose railway was progressing more quickly than Rhodes's. On his advice he bought some donkeys which were immune to epizootic disease and unloaded them at Beira on 28th March. But four days later he learnt that some colonists had been assassinated, a sign that the Matabele revolt had begun. In fact 15,000 natives had surrounded Bulawayo.

As he was no longer on the Board of Chartered he had no official position whatever in the country he had brought into existence. Yet, such is the ascendancy a bold spirit can gain, that, without any right to do so, it was he in fact who directed all the operations. To begin with he commanded the troops and then he prepared the way for negotiation. His first step was to get to the battle area, organise a column and inflict a serious defeat on the Matabeles, who fled to the caves of the Matapos hills. Rhodes did not want to exterminate them but to negotiate, and sent out emissaries to meet them. But the distrustful natives did not come to the rendezvous. So Rhodes, with only a few friends and unarmed, went out and pitched his tent in full view of the caves. The warriors watched him for several days, unable to believe that this display did not conceal a trap.

As soon as the Matabele chieftains were satisfied that Rhodes only wanted to hear what they had to say, they agreed to hold a conference in a place where no armed force could approach them. An invitation was sent to Rhodes by messenger. It meant risking his life, but in his state of mind concern for his reputation outweighed concern for his life. Without a moment's hesitation he mounted his horse and with three companions, all of them unarmed, followed the messenger off into the hills.

At last he found himself confronting the native chieftains, who were surrounded by their fully armed fighters, and listening to their explanation of what had led them to revolt. He argued patiently, offered support for their just claims and secured some concessions from them in return. Finally he asked: " Now, for the future, is it peace or is it war? " For reply, the chieftains dropped their spears on the ground—a sign that the struggle was at an end. As Rhodes and his friends returned to their tent he said: " It is occasions like that which make life worth living."

He and his friends spent two months among the Matabeles, while he urged them: " Go and sow your fields or else you will starve next year." And, let us repeat, Rhodes was nobody at this time; he had resigned from Chartered, and he did not represent the Government. He only had the innate authority of a strong man. That alone was enough to bring the revolt to an end, and on 13th October peace was declared. At his own expense he distributed a million sacks of maize and promised to indemnify the colonists for any loss they had suffered. No one dreamt of telling him that he had no right to engage in these undertakings. He was Cecil Rhodes; that was enough. From this time onwards the natives developed a kind of worship for him and rechristened him " the separator of fighting bulls." This victory, won solely by virtue of his prestige, was the greatest of his life. From the ruins of his career he had emerged with a higher reputation than ever.

When he was ordered back to London in 1897 " to face the music " before the Commission of Enquiry, or, as he put it, " to meet the unctuous rectitude of my countrymen," he was cheered all along the route in South Africa, more as a hero than as one accused. " It is very moving to see one's fellow beings feel so kindly to one. Such appreciation as this usually comes after a man is dead."

In London the first findings of the Commission went all against him. He seemed to be overwhelmed, casting around for words and getting hopelessly lost in a recital of the facts. But it was only a tactical withdrawal, perhaps even a deliberate one. At the afternoon session, having measured up his accusers in the morning, he counter-attacked, showing how, compared with the immensity of his accomplishment and of his services to his country, the charges levelled against him were paltry. Instantly, the public and his judges were on his side. It was only justice that he should be reprimanded but allowed to retain his title of Privy Councillor. He had known from the moment he arrived that it would end like this: " I found all the busmen smiling at me when I came to London, so I knew it was all right." The masses have a greater appreciation for genius than for virtue.

He took advantage of a later visit to Europe to call on the French Minister for Foreign Affairs, Gabriel Hanotaux, in Paris—who describes him as he then saw him, in 1899: large, strong and with square shoulders; a ruddy complexion, red hair and greying side-whiskers and moustache. He looked like a country gentleman, hardened by sport, with a rather imperious air and a direct, almost savage, self-confidence. He told Hanotaux that he was temporarily unthroned, but that he would return to power.

" I have done what was right," he explained. " I have added two thousand miles to my country's length without its costing sixpence. As for you French, I have done my best to help you in Madagascar. . . . You see, the non-civilised races must disappear. You in France must play your part in Africa . . . the future is an alliance between France, Russia and England. No doubt you tell

yourselves I am a fool. But I am not, I am speaking
of the future. What do we look for in this life? To
leave something worth remembering. What does it
matter if I disappear? I have left something to
remember. I have built a country." Hanotaux said
he doubted if it was necessary to wipe out the natives
in order to civilise Africa. " You may be right,"
said Rhodes, " in any case I will help you. There's
no fundamental economic rivalry between France
and England. . . . The real enemy, for both of us,
is Germany." A strange declaration when one
considers the form his will was to take. But we
have yet to see what caused the reversal.

He received a huge ovation on his return to the
Cape. He had now recovered all his old assurance.
He had just learnt of the suicide of his former rival,
Barnato, who had jumped off a boat in mid-ocean
for reasons that were obscure. Rhodes would never
have killed himself—it would have been a confession
of defeat. " My career," he kept saying, " is only
just beginning." All the same, for the future of this
career he was counting more on Rhodesia than on
the Cape.

His house, de Groote Schuur, had burnt down
and he bore this latest disaster stoically: he had it
rebuilt. But he also wanted a house in the Matapos
Hills, with two model farms to be devoted to research
into crops and cattle breeding. He had secured the

co-operation of a Californian expert on the selection and packing of fruit. It was the beginning of another source of enduring wealth to the country. Enterprise was his hobby. Had not his architect, Baker, discovered a seam of brick clay? Rhodes forthwith set up a brickyard, and tile works. Were not the miners crying out for dynamite? He established an explosives factory in Rhodesia and so freed himself of Kruger's monopoly. And were not his visitors becoming so numerous that he could no longer put them up hospitably? He built a hotel.

The Cape to Cairo railway was still his most cherished plan. It was his ardent wish to see it finished before he died. It seemed possible; he was not yet old, but he had taken a lot out of himself, and life was becoming a race against his sick heart. He spurred on the engineers: " We are going on now, to cross the Zambesi at Victoria Falls. I should like to have the spray of the water on the carriages." In 1897 the track reached Bulawayo and in 1898 the telegraph poles were approaching Tanganyika. The whole British world awaited, in a spirit of veneration, the completion of the great track. Rhodes was once more on the Board of Chartered. The Boers of Barkly West had re-elected him. All the implements of power were within his grasp once more, and this had been achieved without abandoning his friends, for Jameson was still at his side, his constant companion.

In 1899 he went to Europe, principally to see two kings: Leopold II, the King of the Belgians, and the Kaiser. He wanted their permission to take his telegraph line over their territory. He found Leopold an obstinate and even aggressive protagonist, but one so persuasive that he won at every round. "Each time I have lunch with him it costs me a province," was Rhodes's description. When all was said and done he did not like Leopold, got nothing from him and summed up the matter with, "Satan, I tell you, that man is Satan." The Kaiser, on the other hand, received him like a friend and, for the most part, gave him what he asked. Rhodes talked to him as man to man and even, in breach of protocol, brought the visit to an end himself: "Well, good-bye," said the Empire builder to the Emperor, "I have to go now as I have some people coming for dinner."

Following his visit to Berlin he spent two or three days at Sandringham, where the Prince of Wales plied him with questions about his interview with the Kaiser. "I liked him," said Rhodes, "because he gave his interest so thoroughly to my ideas, and asked intelligent questions." The Prince of Wales was more chary of the Kaiser's apparent solicitude for the British Empire, and also perhaps of his nephew's supposed intelligence. " You were fortunate, Mr. Rhodes, he is sometimes very difficult." But in the event, when Rhodes notified the Emperor that his telegraph line was approaching the German colonies, and reminded him of the promises he had made, they were faithfully observed. From which sprang Rhodes's lasting gratitude and final testament.

During his visit to England in 1899 he went to Oxford with Kitchener to receive a Doctorate *honoris causa*. No honour could have given greater satisfaction to the passionate admirer of the Oxford system. Oriel, the college to which he had been admitted as a commoner, gave a dinner in his honour, at the end of which he made a speech: " Sometimes, in pursuing my object, the enlargement of the British Empire and with it the cause of peace, industry and freedom, I have adopted means in removing opposition which were the rough and ready way and not the highest way to attain that object. But you must remember that in South Africa where my work has lain, the laws of right and equity are not so fixed and established as in this country. . . . It is among those men that my own life must be weighed and measured." And it is true. The Kimberley miner, " the separator of fighting bulls," could not have been expected to apply, with humility and all perfection, the lessons of the Sunday school.

It is worth mentioning at this point, because of the serious difficulties that Rhodes ran into later as a result of the incident, that, on the boat back to the Cape in the same year, he came across a fully-ripened and divorced Polish princess. Princess Radziwill set her lingering charms in motion in an attempt to conquer the conqueror. She invited his interest by talking to him about international politics, and, after reaching the Cape, made a number of visits to Groote Schuur. She then spread it about that Rhodes was going to marry her. The truth was that he stood in some fear of the lady and had given his intimates instructions never to leave them alone. Events were to show how well-founded was his distrust of her.

* 12 *

War in Africa and the
Death of Rhodes

WHEN RHODES returned to Africa in 1899 the long drawn-out quarrel between the " Uitlanders " and the Boers had become more bitter than ever. Kruger obstinately refused to grant any concessions to the foreigners, who were by now almost in a majority in the Transvaal. The Reformers had grown tired of sending petitions to the Transvaal Government, who simply laughed at them. They appealed instead to Queen Victoria for Britain's support. The brilliant High Commissioner, Sir Alfred Milner, gave them his backing.

On his arrival in South Africa Milner had learnt Dutch and travelled over the whole country. He had come to the conclusion that there would be neither peace nor progress as long as the British of the Transvaal were subjected to the reactionary President. He sent Chamberlain an urgent dispatch, in which he said the English were being treated

" like Helots " and that it was imperative he should intervene. Milner thought the Boers were bluffing and would give way once they were confronted with a strong policy.

However, the Dutch of the Cape and Orange Free State managed to arrange a conference between Kruger and Milner at Bloemfontein. The former asked that all disputes between the Transvaal and Great Britain should be referred to arbitration. Milner insisted that the " Uitlanders " should be entitled to vote after five years' residence. But he failed. Kruger knew that the foreign vote would mean the end of his political power; he did not believe in the military might of Britain, and, remembering his victory over the Jameson raid, was more disposed to fight than to give way. He only wanted to gain time, because by October the grass would be growing on the veld and this would simplify the feeding of his herds and mounted troops. On 27th September, he sent Milner an ultimatum demanding the withdrawal of his troops from the Transvaal frontier and a reply within forty-eight hours. There could be no doubt what the reply would be. Joseph Chamberlain anticipated little risk from such a war. After a short campaign " the Transvaal would be annexed and Sir Alfred would become Lord Milner, two excellent results."

By this time Rhodes was extremely ill. Ever

since the Raid he had had to impose a fierce degree of self-control to conceal his pain. The Matabele war and the reorganisation of Rhodesia had entailed a huge amount of work. He was paying dearly for his strenuous efforts as his strength slowly drained away. He was continually held up in his work by his illness, and this made him irritable. He had always been quick to flare up. But his temper was mostly due to the fact that he knew his time was short. How could he have patience with procrastination, when there was still so much work to be done and so few days to do it? Towards the end, he became so irritable that no one could work with him any longer, except Jameson, who alone knew how to take care of him and calm him. It is absurd to say, as some of his enemies did, that Rhodes and other South African magnates wanted war so as to be able to seize the gold mines. That would have been a contradiction of his whole policy, and besides, he already had the gold mines. In fact, he deliberately kept out of any discussion that might lead to a clash. He simply said, " You can trust Milner." But he was wrong over the strength of the Boers when he said, " Nothing will make Kruger fire a shot." His own adventures should have taught him otherwise—but few men learn from experience.

On the eve of the ultimatum, although in great pain, he decided to go to Kimberley. It was a courageous step, for the Boers had stated that if they took him prisoner they would throw him into a cage of lions. In England, Londoners were singing songs promising Kruger they would eat Christmas dinner with him in Pretoria.

As it turned out things were going very badly by Christmas time. Not only Mafeking and Kimberley, but Ladysmith as well, were besieged. Lord Roberts had just been appointed Commander-in-chief, with Kitchener as his chief of staff, which showed the gravity of the situation. Rhodes as usual displayed impetuous, and sometimes misdirected, energy. He organised canteens, supplied the hospital with fruit from De Beers's orchards, and busied the mine-workers, who had become jobless, with building shelters and planting avenues of pepper trees and eucalyptus. He supplied all volunteers with mounts and equipment, and at De Beers had a big gun, " Long Cecil," made. Its shells bore the message: " Compliments from C.R." War engenders this sort of bravado, and is perhaps an excuse for it.

The trouble was that, though a sincere patriot, he could be subjected to no sort of discipline. He made the life of the colonel commanding Kimberley quite intolerable. He rained messages on the Commander-in-chief demanding that before anything else Kimberley should be relieved, for he had always been unable to appreciate that the general interest did not necessarily coincide with his own. In this respect he had a one-track mind. He even quarrelled with his friend, Kitchener, and in an access of anger demanded the return of the rolling stock which had been lent to the army by his companies. In February 1900 Roberts and Kitchener turned to the offensive with 150,000 men, and on the 13th, following a sabre charge by the cavalry, raised the siege of Kimberley. Rhodes had exasperated the General Staff to such a degree that they refused to enter the town as long as he was there.

In May, Roberts and his army marched on Pretoria. When they reached and occupied Johannesburg Kruger fled from his capital to Europe in a Dutch warship, taking his secret papers with him. Some reproached him for deserting his followers, while others held that he was right to try to enlist the support of friendly powers in favour of two small nations who were supposed to be fighting for their freedom. It was a barely tenable argument, for, as we know, Kruger was no respecter of freedom in his own land, but in 1901 the Tsar wrote to Edward VII saying his conscience was troubled by the war. For that matter the Tsar was hardly a good judge of liberty.

The Boer generals, Botha, Smuts and De Wet, had decided to wage continuous guerrilla warfare while Kruger tried, in vain, as it turned out, to secure the intervention of a European power. Roberts had declared the war won and on 25 October 1900 the ceremony of annexing the Transvaal took place at Pretoria.   At the time Kipling was in Bloemfontein publishing a paper for the troops. Roberts left South Africa and Kitchener remained in command.   But nothing is harder than holding a rebellious country where every farmer is an enemy.   How were partisans to be prevented from attacking isolated detachments, capturing convoys and blowing up the railway?   The war had degenerated into a large-scale police operation, but was still costly in men and materials.

What was to be done?   Rhodes, speaking at a victory dinner in Cape Town, tried to explain.   With his eyes fixed on Table Mountain, he spoke like a man in a trance of his old dream of union: " You think you have beaten the Dutch!   But it is not so. The Dutch are not beaten . . . No!   The Dutch are as vigorous and unconquered to-day as they have ever been;   the country is still as much theirs as it is yours and you will have to live and work with them hereafter as in the past . . . let there be no vaunting words, no vulgar triumph over your Dutch neighbours;   make them feel that bitterness is past and that the need of co-operation is greater than ever."   He moved his audience.   It was the great Rhodes, the Separator of Fighting Bulls, suddenly emerging from a broken body.

A return to public office was offered to him at this time, but he had neither the strength nor the inclination for it. A morbid agitation drove him from place to place looking for somewhere that could make him feel better. He visited his farms, his orchards, his railways, his gold mines and his diamond mines; or else he would say to friends: " Let's go away and have our chop on the veld." Then, having spent the whole day shooting, he would sit round a camp fire in the evening, surrounded by his old friends, and go over the stories of the past; and, as they sipped Nyasaland coffee, he would recapture his youth. But insomnia followed. He could neither restrain himself from ceaseless activity, nor rest.

He had drawn up his will. Kipling was now at " The Woolsack " and Rhodes often came down to expand on his ideas for the scholarships with the poet and his wife. As always he had difficulty in finding the right words. He was aware of his inadequacy. " What am I trying to express? " he would ask Kipling, who has left a description of the scene: " ' Say it, say it,' Rhodes would command, so I would say it, and if the phrase suited not, he would work it over, chin a little down, till it satisfied him."

At last the will was completed. He left Groote Schuur, with a considerable sum for its upkeep, as a residence for the Prime Minister of the Cape. With his immense fortune he endowed a foundation which was to award £300 scholarships every year to young men of the British Dominions and Colonies, and of the United States. Brought together, generation after generation, he hoped " Rhodes Scholars " would draw tighter the links which bind the British Empire and the Anglo-Saxon world.

" I desire to encourage and foster an appreciation of the advantage which I implicitly believe will result from the union of the English-speaking people throughout the world." In recognition of the good will shown him by Kaiser William II he also created, by codicil, some scholarships for young Germans, to be awarded by the Kaiser. He said he thought he would be furthering the cause of peace by giving young Germans an opportunity of knowing England. This faith in the civilising influence of Oxford, this confidence in the beneficent power of the classics, show that after all his struggles the old warrior had not abandoned the beliefs of his youth. His will, and the hopes he based on it, softened the pain of his last years: " It is the pleasantest companion I have."

Otherwise, everything round him gave cause for anguish. In spite of the occupation of the main towns, the war between those he wished to see united was still in progress. It had taken a cruel turn, which is what happens when a regular army has to defend itself against guerrillas. Many English people were shocked to see Christians fighting each other with such bitterness. But in reality the battle was less fierce than it appeared from a distance. The Boers were fighting like hunters, the English like sportsmen. Neither side felt the game would be won or lost until hands were raised in complete surrender, and so this petty war disintegrated into a rather childish game on horseback. It was from the Transvaal that Baden Powell drew his inspiration for the Boy Scout movement.

But Rhodes, becoming progressively more ill, was horrified by the political and military mess and distracted by the struggle between English and Boer, whose union had been the great hope of his life. For the first time he travelled without any object in view, simply to escape a terrible spectacle. He went to Italy, then to Egypt where he studied cotton-growing with Rhodesia in mind, and lastly to England where he bought a house in Norfolk. Then he was forced to return to Africa because of a distressing law case. The regrettable Princess Radziwill had forged his signature on a cheque for £29,000 and was brought to account.

He left England for the last time on 18 February

1902 to come and give evidence, and reached the Cape at the height of the hot season, which was a menace to his weak heart. To get him a slight breeze Jameson found him a cottage by the sea at Muizenberg. For some time he dragged himself out in the afternoons to visit Groote Schuur in the motor car he had brought back from England. It was the first one in South Africa and he was naïvely proud of it. But soon he could no longer get up. Jameson nursed him day and night with absolute devotion and, to give him more air, had two holes made in the ceiling and an extra window put in. But neither the ventilation nor pails of ice could calm his fever.

Unable to sleep, he would harp endlessly on his unfinished work and the towns in the countries he had built. A great tree-lined avenue was to be built at Bulawayo—" See it through. Trees . . . Trees . . . Plant trees." Then he became obsessed with a wish to see England again, and had cabins reserved in a boat leaving on 26th March. He especially wanted to see Oxford, and one day a visitor recited the passage from Matthew Arnold on Oxford, " Beautiful city, so venerable, so lovely." Rhodes lifted himself up, enchanted to the point of forgetting his pain: " Go on . . . go on . . . quote the whole passage."

On the 25th a telegram came from Kitchener,

who had long since ranged himself on his side in favour of a generous peace and a broadly-based amnesty. The General announced that at long last the Boers were ready to enter into negotiations: "Thank God," said Rhodes, when he read it, "I hope the right leaders will be chosen to frame a lasting peace." The following afternoon, just as Jameson had gone to lie down, exhausted, Rhodes suddenly muttered: "So little done, so much to do." Then in a loud, clear voice he called out for Jameson. But when the doctor reached him, Cecil Rhodes was dead.

In 1896, while he had been settling the Matabele revolt, he had discovered in the Matapos hills, forty-five miles from Bulawayo, a mound of rock standing up in the middle of a prodigiously wide stretch of green and wild country. He fell in love with it. "I call this one of the world's views," he had said, and, ever since, his friends had called the hill "the view of the world." Nearby was the tomb of King Mozelikatze, who had asked to be buried in a sitting position at this, the highest, point in his kingdom, so that even in death he could look at the magnificent vista before him. "What a poet," Rhodes had exclaimed, and he had stipulated that he also wished to be buried there.

Thus, on 3 April 1902, a train bearing his body left Cape Town for Rhodesia. All the way along, in

the doorways of farms, on station platforms, silent
groups of Boers and English were gathered to pay
tribute to the country's founder.   On the 8th he
reached Bulawayo, and the coffin was laid in the
stoep of his farm, from which he had loved to gaze
at the mountains.   The next day a gun-carriage
drawn by twelve oxen carried him off to the hills.

On reaching the Matapos region thousands of
Matabeles met him, crying " *Bayete* "—the greeting
traditionally accorded to their kings.   When the
coffin was lowered into the tomb, they chanted a
funeral hymn.   And then Faku, one of the chieftains,
spoke: " I am an old man on the brink of the
grave.   I was content to die knowing that my
children and my people would be safe in the hands
of Mr. Rhodes, who was at once my father and
mother.   That hope has been taken from me and I
feel that the sun, indeed, has set for me."

The funeral and the tomb were on the scale of
the man.   Cecil Rhodes was a giant and it would
not seem right, at the end of his stupendous adventure, to measure him by the same standards as
ordinary men.   Ambitious?   Yes, of course, he was
ambitious.   " I would annex the planets and the
stars if I could," he said.   It would be easy to
judge him harshly, to reproach him for his love of
absolute power, his insensitiveness and complete

lack of scruple where business was concerned. The unctuous rectitude, to which he referred with such contempt, could easily be applied to him, but it would also be unfair. He was a great man.

In the pioneer who read Marcus Aurelius, in the gold digger who looked for ancient wisdom, there was no trace of vulgarity. His aim, of extending the British Empire by means of self-governing federations, because he believed the Empire was an instrument for civilisation, was disinterested. A millionaire without personal needs, he had built a fortune not to provide himself with mediocre pleasures, but to build a new world. " I never tried to make money for its own sake," he once said. It was true. Passionately English, he had none the less called for friendship between all races. In South Africa he had defended the rights of Afrikaners and natives. His generous motives must be put to his credit. In his long conflict with Kruger, it was after all on Rhodes's side that the just solution for South Africa's future was to be found.

Also to his credit are the beautiful countries which bear his name and whose prosperity justifies the determination he showed in founding them. " In this square at Salisbury where, sixty years ago, Rhodes might be seen shaving outside his tent, to-day illuminated fountains play." Salisbury, five thousand feet above sea level, and Bulawayo, with its average sunshine of eight hours a day, both offer thousands of European families an ideal climate. These great towns, which are scarcely colonial, remind one far more of Texan cities than of Brazzaville or Dakar. " Rhodes and his dreams are still a factor in an ever-changing world." People walk under the shade of the trees he planted, and never saw.

As Rhodes was dying in the appalling heat, at the cottage near Cape Town, he had looked incessantly and with longing towards " his North." Perhaps the dreamer in him saw beyond the veld and beyond the battles with hostile tribes, to the British countries and the white communities who inhabit them, and owe everything to him. And perhaps we, having retraced his thrilling, wild and passionate life, can understand why the tombstone in the Matapos Hills, watched over by gigantic boulders in the middle of a strangely green and untouched scene, is now an object of pilgrimage by many men from many lands. Greatness is not the same as virtue, but there is always virtue in it.

Chronological Table

1852		Britain recognised independence of Transvaal
1853	July 5	Cecil Rhodes born
1854		Britain recognises independence of Orange Free State
1867		First diamond found in South Africa
1870		Rhodes lands in South Africa for first time
		Discovery of Kimberley dry diggings
1871		Rhodes goes to diamond fields
1873	Oct. 13	Rhodes admitted to Oriel College, Oxford
1877		Transvaal annexed
1879		Zulu War
1880	Nov.	Rhodes elected for Barkly West
	Dec.	Transvaal War began
1881	Feb. 27	Majuba
		Independence restored to Transvaal
	Dec. 17	Rhodes takes B.A. and M.A.
1886		Gold discovered on Witwatersrand
1887		Amalgamation of De Beers claims
		Foundation of Goldfields of South Africa
1888		Almalgamation of De Beers and Kimberley, as De Beers Consolidated Mines
1889		British South Africa Co. granted Royal Charter of Incorporation
1890		Rhodes Prime Minister of the Cape
		The march of the pioneer column on Mashonaland
1893		The Matabele War
1895	Dec. 29	The Jameson Raid
1896	Jan. 5	Rhodes resigns Premiership
	June 26	Rhodes resigns from Board of " Chartered "
		The Matabele Rebellion
1897		Rhodes before South Africa Committee
1898		Rhodes restored to Board of " Chartered "
1899/1902		The South African War
1902	Mar. 26	Death of Rhodes
1904		Death of Kruger
1909		Union of South Africa Act

A Note on Sources

My main authorities for this book were:

BASIL WILLIAMS: *Cecil Rhodes* (London, Constable & Co., 1921).

J. G. MACDONALD: *Rhodes* (London, Philip Allan & Co., 1927).

STUART CLOETE: *African Portraits* (London, Collins, 1946).

SCULLY: *Reminiscences of a South African Pioneer.*

SIR LEWIS MICHELL: *Life of the Right Honourable C. J. Rhodes.*

W. D. GALE: *Heritage of Rhodes* (Oxford University Press, 1950).

Numerous articles have been published in French magazines between 1870 and 1900, on the discovery of diamond mines and on early life at Kimberley. I made great use of them. Hanotaux's account is from the *Revue des Deux Mondes*. André Blanchet's articles on Rhodesia were published in *Le Monde*.

A. M.

Brief Lives

" A notable new series of short biographies "
EDMUND BLUNDEN

SIR FRANCIS DRAKE
J. A. WILLIAMSON

" Williamson is the real authority on Elizabethan sea-
manship, and has a great gift in choosing what is
important to tell and telling it clearly in very few words."
G. M. TREVELYAN

QUEEN VICTORIA
ROGER FULFORD

" The clearest, best-balanced, and most understanding
life of the Queen yet written." ARTHUR BRYANT

MONTROSE
C. V. WEDGWOOD

" This short book captures better than any that I have
read, the excitement, the tragic poetry, of his brief,
dramatic career." ROSE MACAULAY

QUEEN ELIZABETH I
MILTON WALDMAN

"He has carried out his task brilliantly, selecting and summarising with fine judgment, and presenting vividly Elizabeth as woman, politician, and Queen."

YORKSHIRE POST

ABRAHAM LINCOLN
HERBERT AGAR

"I do not know of any book which gives so compact and comprehensible a picture of this extraordinary man."

EDWARD SHANKS

RUPERT OF THE RHINE
BERNARD FERGUSSON

"The author of *Beyond the Chindwin* and *The Wild Green Earth* gives a stirring account of the life and career of the great cavalry leader and opponent of Cromwell."

CHATHAM
J. H. PLUMB

The dramatic story of the great eighteenth century statesman, whose proud boast "I know that I can save the country and that I alone can" was so brilliantly vindicated.